DANCE INTO LIFE

INSIGHTS AND PERSPECTIVES
ON GOING FOR YOUR DREAMS

This book is dedicated to everyone who loves dance,
the performing arts, and show business.

www.danceintolifebook.com

First Printing, 2018 – Printed in Canada

ISBN 978-0-9755437-2-6

TABLE OF CONTENTS

FOREWORD 2

INTRODUCTION. AND... CURTAIN 3

SECTION 1.
FINDING DIRECTION

1. What Do You Want from Life? 9
2. Know Thyself 15
3. The Power of the Mind 19

SECTION 2.
DANCE EDUCATION

4. The Splendors of Dance 25
5. The Right Dance Studio 29
6. If You're Lucky, You Attend Dance Conventions ... 33
7. Sign Me Up for Competitions... or Not 35
8. Training Through the Years 37

SECTION 3.
A CAREER IN DANCE

9. Dance as a Way of Life 43
10. Relocation Navigation 45
11. Auditioning 49
12. Representation: Agents and Managers 53
13. Unions and Other Support Organizations 59
14. Careers Behind the Curtain 61
15. Dance Studio Ownership 65

SECTION 4.
PERSONAL POWER

16. Higher Education 71
17. Health Is Wealth 75
18. It's About Time 81
19. Let's Talk Money 87
20. Mind Over Manners 91
21. Character Matters 97
22. Who You Run With 99

SECTION 5.
HELP AND INSPIRATION

23. Finding Your Mentors 103
24. What I Wish I Had Known 105
25. In Case You Didn't Know 115

SECTION 6.
DANCE INTO LIFE

26. You Have a Voice... Use It 129
27. Your Art Comes to Life Through You 133
28. Treat Yourself to Life 135
29. And Another Thing 139

FOREWORD

This is, without a doubt, a great book you have in your hands. It represents the future of all that is possible for you in the arts and entertainment industry. It is a resource not only about show business, but also about a way of understanding how to push yourself to do what you love without boundaries, thereby allowing you to forge new frontiers. This book helps you transform what you thought was possible for your life into a reality by incorporating timeless life principles—principles that have afforded me much success, both personally and professionally.

I knew that Joe Tremaine and Laurie Johnson had incredible wisdom to share. They have proved that by passing on their expertise for many years. I wasn't prepared, however, for them to drive home their points with such personal anecdotes and life lessons. It is an important and honest work that speaks to all of us. I love it! Their stories are infused with passion and the desire to make a difference. I know they will give you the inspiration to make a breakthrough with your own personal performance.

There is something for everyone here. So as you read these pages, apply the content that is relevant to your own particular life. The hope is that you are inspired to unlock your extraordinary power and lead our industry to even grander heights.

In my travels around the globe and as I watch the performing arts evolve, I take note of our leaders who have experienced and learned so much. Who better to learn from? I'm excited for any artist brave enough to step out and share their gifts with the world. I honor the next generation of revolutionary leaders making the next bold moves.

Everything you need to create a great future lies within YOU! This book will help you find it and thereby... .... bloom wherever you are planted.

~ Nigel Lythgoe

INTRODUCTION. AND... CURTAIN

The best ideas start as conversations.

~ Jonathan Ive

Laurie: Top of the morning to you, Mr. Tremaine. How are you today?

Joe: Pure perfection.

Laurie: I expected no less.

Joe: You know, I've been thinking... that all of us, no matter what we do on a daily basis, are in show business in one way or another.

Laurie: So true.

Joe: For you and me, the thing we love just happens to be show business, but it could be anything. It doesn't matter. You still have to get up, dress up, show up, and go to where the action is to get in the game.

Laurie: I love the fact that we're actually in it and that we found ways to stay close to what we love. And now, we participate day to day or at least weekly in what we enjoy.

Joe: To think that most of us pretty much start out the same way, at our local dance studios. We do plié at the barre and from that pointe on, there's no limit to what we can accomplish.

Laurie: I know, right? There's so much we can do through dance. It paves the way to endless possibilities.

Joe: Well, I for one am thankful that I work—if you can really call it that—at something I love to do. Don't get me wrong, I put in long hours and am dog-tired sometimes. But when you're doing what you want and what you love to do, it's not work at all.

Laurie: It might not be easy, but it certainly is rewarding and well worth the effort.

Joe: That's why I tell people, "Go for your dreams. And if a career in dance is something you want, what's holding you back? Nothing."

Laurie: Touché, my good man, touché.

Joe: We should write a book about this.

Laurie: Mr. Tremaine, I'm in.

So we did. We wrote a book about how sweet life is when you spend time at the intersection where life collides with dance.

We remember what it was like to wonder where to start, what to do next, and whom to ask for help. We remember asking ourselves, "How am I going to make it and can I really build a life and a living around my artistry?"

In planning our book, we thought *choreography*. And with any choreography, you want to engage audiences with something unique and memorable. You don't want to bore people or waste their time by doing just any ol' steps, flips, or tricks to some random song.

So, we structured our content around real-life storytelling. When you see this icon,  you'll know you've come upon Joe Tremaine's stories, comments, advice, and/or humor.

When  @laurietalks, you'll see her icon. The two of us share our perspectives, experiences, and the practical ideas we've learned about life, hoping it will make *your* life a little easier.

Our book is part encouragement, part business guide, and part show business inspiration. Here's a glimpse at some of the content staged in the twenty-nine chapters.

Work-life balance topics relate to mentorship, procrastination, time and money management, health as your ultimate wealth, and the art of getting things done.

The discussion on propriety and protocol speaks to presenting yourself with aplomb. Think: integrity, tact, civility, social graces, who you run with, and raising the barre on your reputation.

Topics associated with knowing who you are, standing up for yourself, and keeping the green-eyed monster at bay have a common theme: the power of positive thinking.

The "What I Wish I Had Known" chapter includes input from over seventy individuals. Some represent the who's who of our industry. Others—not as well known or as well established, but who get up, dress up, and show up in the game every day— also weigh in.

We asked studio owners across the country for their input on what the next generation of owners should know. The chapter titled "Dance Studio Ownership" is a compilation of their responses.

Just as important as where you're going is where you've been. "In Case You Didn't Know" comprises 150-plus basic, insightful questions about show business history. What's presented is but a small sampling of categories, subjects, facts, and figures from our industry's rich culture. We implore you to research, on your own those areas of interest to you.

JOE TREMAINE'S
STORIES,
COMMENTS,
ADVICE, AND/OR
HUMOR

LAURIE JOHNSON'S
STORIES,
COMMENTS,
ADVICE, AND/OR
HUMOR

Who's Going to Benefit from Our Book? We wanted to sit down—virtually, via this book—with two categories of dancers.

1 **Those Who Want Only to Dance and/or Perform** – Many variables are at play. There's a lot to manage and even more to discover. But, yes, you can build a career that connects your life to dance and show business. Check out the chapters titled "Training Through the Years," "Auditioning," "Your Art Comes To Life Through You," and "Dance as a Way of Life."

2 **Those Who Love Dance, But Want to Explore and Employ Their Non-Dance-Related Interests** – Not everyone has the drive, desire, or stamina to dance and rehearse for hours on end, or perform eight or more shows a week. Nor is everyone certain about doing just one thing for the rest of his or her life. Your dance training is a springboard to a lifetime of never-ending career opportunities.

If you left off dancing some time ago, or are transitioning out of the performance world, you don't have to turn your back on dance—or divide your interests, abandoning one part of you to blossom in another.

The chapter "Careers Behind the Curtain" lists fields and areas that at first glance may seem unrelated to dance but in actuality are dance-adjacent. Use this chapter to connect the dots and thus gain insight into how your other interests might relate to dance.

GET ACQUAINTED WITH YOUR AUTHORS.

Joe Tremaine began dancing when he was four years old and was teaching dance before he graduated high school. He attended University of Louisiana at Monroe (formerly Northeast Louisiana University). After college, he trained and performed with the New Orleans Ballet Association and the New Orleans Opera before heading north to New York City. See Joe Tremaine's story, "Steps on Broadway," in the chapter "Relocation Navigation."

In 1967, a job on *The Jerry Lewis Show* brought him to Los Angeles. He established Tremaine Dance Center in 1970 and played a part in what came to be known as West Coast jazz. At his studio, Joe offered 115 classes a week, the majority of them taught by LA's best. His students included many of the "big names" in entertainment at the time. Celebrities such as Raquel Welch, Helen Hunt, Paula Abdul, and even Marcia Clark, the famous prosecuting attorney, took classes at his studio.

DANCE
TRAINING
IS LIFE
TRAINING.

After almost thirty years of teaching, performing, and choreographing for stage, television, and film, Joe decided it was time to devote more effort to growing Tremaine Dance Conventions—and that he did. The floor-to-ceiling bookcases in his North Hollywood office display hundreds of trophies, plaques, crystal awards, certifications, and accolades which, taken as a whole, represent decades of success as a dancer and business owner. He's been honored by a New York City mayor and a governor of Louisiana.

"Dance training is life training," says Joe Tremaine, and his life is the proof. He turned his penchant for movin' and groovin' into a million-dollar dance convention empire. Not easy. Thank goodness he had help. In 1981, he established Tremaine Dance Conventions with Julie Adler, his savvy business partner. Adler held it down in her day and was an active and crucial force in managing the company for the first thirty years.

If you're fortunate enough to be one of the 60,000 dancers, teachers, and parents who attend Tremaine Dance Conventions annually, it's possible you've spotted Joe, a dance bag on his shoulder regardless of whether he's headed to a gala, a pre-con business meeting, dinner, or to host an evening of competition. Trivia: Over the past thirty-six years, Joe Tremaine has attended roughly 800 winter and summer city conventions. That's a lot of LAX take-offs and landings.

At the Capezio A.C.E. Awards, Joe received *DanceTeacher*'s 2017 Award of Distinction. According to Cathy Roe, a fellow convention owner, Joe Tremaine has "inspired people to the point of cultural change explosion."

This shy, skinny kid from the cotton fields of Louisiana followed, accomplished, and exceeded his dreams, all while inspiring countless other dancers to do the same.

Laurie Johnson is the daughter of a dance studio owner. Her first dream was to be a politician, but after serving as a Congressional intern for the United States House of Representatives, she changed her mind.

Her corporate life in management at MCI Worldcom and later at the Sara Lee Corporation proved empty without dance. Laurie filled the void by giving up her high-profile, six-figure, Fortune 500 salary. She traded pumps for tap shoes, stuffy suits for costumes, and corporate business for show business.

In 1998, a year after relocating to Los Angeles, she landed a faculty position with Tremaine Dance Conventions. This was a direct result of being not only in the right place at the right time, but also ready. For particulars on creating your own luck through preparation—getting ready to meet opportunity—check out Laurie's story "Bye-Bye, Corporate America; Hello, Hollywood" in the chapter "What Do You Want from Life?"

Laurie's two previous books, *Rich by Choice, Poor by Habit* (2004) and *TAP IN to Your Full Potential* (2008), are awesome. In 2015, she won, by national voters' choice, the Industry Dance Awards title "Favorite Dance Convention Teacher."

@Laurietalks blogs at lauriejohnson.com, hosts talk radio for dancers, loves Toastmasters International, and is a Certified Life Coach and a proud member of the National Speakers Association. Her message is twofold. Keep life simple and shake off what you don't need—especially mediocrity.

Laurie has a BA from The George Washington University and an MBA from The University of Texas at Austin.

She is the crafty designer of her very own custom, handmade, one-of-a-kind, attention-grabbing, rhinestone-studded tap shoes.

Back in the day, Laurie traveled to Guinea, West Africa for an intense Djembe (drumming) internship with Les Percussions de Guinea and Les Ballet Africains. She then toured the U.S. with two of her sisters in a tapping and drumming trio called "Three Sisters Tappin." Since her sisters no longer dance, today Laurie is a sister tapping. The end. ◆

Although we've been toiling in the furrows for quite some time, we don't have all the answers—nor are we trying to teach you anything. Instead, our goal in writing Dance into Life is to cheer you on, and to remind you to honor and appreciate what makes you special—which, by the way, is why we're glad you're here.

The dream you have for yourself is the same dream we have for you. It's the same one both of us had for ourselves when we were trying to find ways to make dance like breakfast—part of our everyday lives.

Allow us to pull back the curtain and give you a behind-the-scenes peek at some of what we've learned at the crossroads of dance and life. Show time.

—Joe and Laurie

THE DREAM YOU HAVE FOR YOURSELF IS THE SAME DREAM WE HAVE FOR YOU.

SECTION 1
FINDING DIRECTION

1. WHAT DO YOU WANT FROM LIFE?

*There is a law in psychology that if you form a picture in your mind
of what you would like to be, and you keep and hold that picture there
long enough, you will soon become exactly as you have been thinking.*

~ William James

Remember kindergarten? You probably answered questions about your future—including "What do you want to be when you grow up?"—without much thinking. Kids, who tend to worry less, don't consider complications or consequences to the point that it stops them from dreaming big and believing.

Some adults look back on their childhood interests to help guide them toward a path they love. Connect with your inner child as a discovery option for learning more about yourself. Recall the fearlessness and determination of your childlike nature. If a kid wants to put footprints on the moon, the challenges of space travel could very well act as motivation.

Facing North. As a teenager, I used to sit in my backyard and face north. I'd literally turn my body northward because in that direction lay New York City. My hope was that I would somehow magically transport myself there. That's how desperately I wanted to dance in the big city. Crazy, right? Not really, because it happened exactly as I imagined it would. I was determined to make it as a dancer and live a show-business kind of life. ✦

Let's Just Wait and See What Happens. When I was 12 years old, my brother Kevin approached me with a deck of cards and an offer to play a game with him called "52 Card Pickup." I was ecstatic that he wanted to spend time with me. "Yes!" I said. As I sat down to play, my brother threw the entire deck across the room with all his might. He laughed as the cards scattered everywhere.

Today, when I hear someone say, "Let's just wait and see what happens," I think about that game—and also about this Ben Franklin quote: "Some people die at 25 and aren't buried until 75."

Those who toss their lives up with a wait-and-see-how-things-land approach miss out on all the fun involved in playing the hand they're dealt. There's only so much bluffing we can do before ultimately having to play or fold.

Decisions about what to do day to day may not always be obvious, but to have no direction is to have no destination. Raise the stakes and ante up on your life. Consider what Glinda, the Good Witch of the North, advised Dorothy: "You had the power all along, my dear." And, consider this fact: You can formulate an ideal for yourself. Let this fact be enough proof that you have the capacity to achieve your ideal *you*. ✦

LIFE
DEALS
YOU A
HAND.
**YOU
CONTROL
THE PLAY.**

READY, SET, GOAL.

Goals provide direction—and a way for you to see beyond today's wants. They're the challenges you set for yourself and the *why* behind your actions. Here's some advice for setting them.

- Be *specific*. Vague goals produce vague results.
- Break goals down into small, achievable parts. Ginormous goals can squash your confidence because they're overwhelming, while puny goals may limit your motivation because they're too easy to attain.
- Resist trying to achieve too many goals at once, which wastes time and is unproductive.

Think with Ink: Part 1. Goal-setting experts consistently talk about the importance of writing down your goals and reviewing them often. Great things happen between the hand and the head. Writing clarifies your thoughts the way movement clarifies choreography. The simple act of writing down what you want implies that you believe it's attainable.

Think with Ink: Part 2. Write down what you want, then work on it more than you talk about it. I can remember choreography like nobody's business. But for everything else, I have to write it down. That's how I stay organized. I write everything down. (I probably should have bought stock in companies that manufacture yellow legal pads. I use them every day and have done so forever.)

Staying organized is how I live my life and get things done. At night, I list and prioritize what needs to happen, and then I sleep in peace knowing exactly what's ahead for me the next day. I have an agenda—a plan—and I do the important stuff first. In the same way you can't walk onstage to perform with no music, no vision, no direction, and no choreography, you can't live each day with no direction.

My favorite book on this subject is aptly titled *Write It Down, Make It Happen,* by Henriette Anne Klauser. I love this book and keep a copy in my office. I recommend it often... much like I'm doing right now. ✦

I LIST AND PRIORITIZE WHAT NEEDS TO HAPPEN, AND THEN I SLEEP IN PEACE KNOWING EXACTLY WHAT'S AHEAD FOR ME THE NEXT DAY.

WRITE ON.

On a piece of paper, in your journal, or on an electronic device, complete the following statements. Number each response with the number of the statement.

Check back periodically to review what you've written, and make adjustments if your goals change—or, if you've achieved those goals, write new ones. To activate the laws of expectation, write your responses in present-tense language.

1. I want to_____.
(What is your goal?)

2. I could totally achieve this by _____.
(Set a realistic deadline.)

3. One thing I can do right now to help me reach this goal is to _____.
(What is your first move?)

4. Then, over the next few months, I can _____**and**

_____.
(Set mini-goals.)

5. Even if _____ **happens,**
(Predict some potential pitfalls.)

I won't give up because _____.
(Be your own cheerleader!)

WHAT WOULD YOU DO IF YOU WERE NOT AFRAID?

Have you ever acted in spite of fear and then later looked back and acknowledged, "Oh, that wasn't so bad"?

If you suspect there's something holding you back from taking action toward creating what you want, then responding to the statements below may provide you with insight. Sometimes, the simple act of identifying what you fear can get you into gear. Complete the following statements on a piece of paper, in your journal, or on an electronic device, numbering each response with the number of the statement, as you did before.

1) I really want to .... *(Name one thing you seriously want to do.)*
Earn my SAG-AFTRA card, earn a living as a dancer, travel the world, achieve triple-threat status, go (back) to college, relocate, learn a new language, perform on Broadway, make my parents proud, live with no regrets.

2) But, I hold back because I'm afraid .... *(Be honest.)*
I'll fail, I'll succeed, I'll look foolish, others will judge me, I'll love it and still not be happy, I'll be unfulfilled, I'll regret I didn't start sooner, it will be too hard, I'll think I'm not good enough (or smart enough).

3) I believe in myself and I know I have what it takes, but I keep thinking ..... *(List all the reasons why you've put off getting started.)*
I'll start next week, I'll wait until I'm in better shape, I'll wait until I save more money, I can't do this alone, maybe I need more training, this might be the wrong move, I'm supposed to be doing something else instead, my friends and family won't understand, my family needs me right now, this is a terrible time of year to move (or start something new).

4) The worst thing that could happen is that I ...... *(Use your imagination.)*
Fail, get injured, make mistakes, give it my all and still not book work, do everything right and still have things go wrong, discover I want something different, realize I've been holding myself back.

5) If that happens, then what? ...... *(You've reached your moment of truth.)*
I will have fallen down, learned from my missteps, and proven I'm human.

Nothing but Net. I'm extremely comfortable jumping right in. Because if I think too much on a subject, I'll become inundated with "what-ifs" and talk myself out of taking action. Pesky details overwhelm me and cause mind chaos.

This is why I begin a lot of projects with no endgame or exit strategy. When I plan vacations, I only book airfare. I trust that lodging, ground transportation, dining, and other activities will all fall into place. They usually do. I paint rooms without using a drop cloth, tape, or a backing-out-of-the room strategy. (Afterwards, I spend more time backtracking and cleaning than I spent painting the room.) I unbox, plug in, and start playing with electronics before glancing at the directions. And there's this crazy rumor going around that I walk onstage to teach a dance convention class and ask, "O.K. Who's got music?"

I take leaps of faith, believing the net will appear. Planning takes too much spontaneity out of life for my taste. This approach isn't for everyone, and I don't recommend it. It can cause sensations of free-falling and periods of wondering if one's parachute will ever open.

My parachute does open, but not always smoothly. Sometimes I'm flying and gliding—a lot—by faith, and free-falling along the way. From some miserable parts of life, I've experienced an ulcer, sleepless nights, bald spots on my head, tearful journal entries, a sad heart, and 20 extra pounds. Yet no matter how turbulent my journey gets, I hold on to faith because that's what gets me past *What if?* or *I'm scared* or *I might look crazy.* Even the most turbulent of flights leads to a beautiful destination. And where there's faith, there's power . . . and failure has no power over faith, right?

What motivates you to give your life your all? For me, it's tap dancing and show business. Whether yours is parenting, public service, or being a frontline employee, mega CEO, dance teacher, or pop star, find and latch onto what gets you riled up and ecstatic at the same time.

Leap at your own speed, believing you can fly using the strength of your own wings. Grand jeté, flea hop, or over the top and back essence—it's your choice. Trust yourself. Be patient with yourself, and anticipate smooth landings. ✦

WHY YOU WANT WHAT YOU WANT.

Your *why* is the power generator that keeps you interested, engaged, and going, even when no one is watching. Your *why* is the force that joyfully drives you and gets you out of bed in the morning . . . and keeps you tirelessly working just one more hour past the time you want to go to sleep.

Ask and It Is Given. People receive astounding benefits simply by asking for them. Yet surprisingly, asking—one of the most powerful success tools of all—is a challenge for many. If you're not asking, ask yourself why not.

Some people don't ask because they don't want to appear needy or foolish. Others are afraid of getting a *no* for an answer and being rejected.

Those who don't ask in essence say *no* to themselves before anyone else has the chance. Don't assume that you're going to be told *no.* And if you aren't told *yes,* you're no worse off than when you began.

Ask, Believing. Ask someone who has the power to say *yes,* and ask as if you expect to get what you want. Be clear. Be reasonable.

You don't ask, you don't get. It's that simple. Whether you want to get a raise, a donation, a room with a view, a discount, a free trial class, top-secret information, a hot date, a more convenient appointment time, time off, a late checkout, help with choreography, or an extension on paying a bill, the very act of asking speaks to your willingness to potentially withstand rejection.

Bye-Bye, Corporate America; Hello, Hollywood. In 1998 I moved to Los Angeles to tap dance. Yet, for the first couple of months I told myself, "Do not take a tap class. Do not take a tap class." I knew that if I showed up as a student, I'd be viewed as a student—and then I'd have to earn the right to teach.

I didn't have that kind of time. Besides, I'd been teaching tap since I was a 12-year-old at my mother's dance studio. I was already a teacher and moving to a new city didn't change that fact. People categorize other people. If I'd taken a tap class, yes, it's likely I would have been a great student, but that wasn't my goal. I wanted a different kind of teaching experience. I needed to make more money than an average class rate. I had no plans to work 40 hours a week running from studio to studio to teach tap in places that were located along a parking lot of a freeway called the I-405. I wanted efficiency. I wanted to teach fewer hours yet make enough to support myself. Then, during the times when I wasn't in the classroom teaching, I would look for other ways to generate income.

A fresh start is permission to introduce yourself to your new world as the person you want to be. I deliberately showed people what I wanted them to see. On the surface, I seemed to have it all together. Yet deep down, life in a new city had me apprehensive, overwhelmed, scared, and wondering how I was going to make it.

There were no GPS apps back then, so I bought a *Thomas Guide* for $22, completely baffled as to why a map would cost so much. While turning the pages of my expensive map, I spotted the name of a town that hinted at a possible location for dance studios. (I later learned that Studio City was named for a movie studio lot. Today, CBS, NBC, Universal, Disney, and Warner Bros have studios in the area.)

> A FRESH START
> IS PERMISSION
> TO INTRODUCE
> YOURSELF TO
> YOUR NEW
> WORLD AS THE
> PERSON YOU
> WANT TO BE.

I visited every dance studio in Studio City. In each one, I walked in, handed a business card to a desk manager, and offered to sub any tap class. Within a week, Lynn Givens, the manager of a place I thought was called The Dance Center, phoned asking me to do just that.

I was beyond excited to finally lace up my kicks. Toward the end of class, I spotted a tall, blue-eyed, debonair gentleman observing me hit the wood. I later found out that he owned the studio, called Tremaine Dance Center. He approached me, and this happened...

MR. DEBONAIR: Hello. My name is Joe Tremaine. Have you ever taught at a dance convention?
ME: Sir, I've never even heard of a dance convention. But I love to teach, and I'm very good at it.

YOUR
TALENTS
HAVE
POWER.

YOUR
GOALS ARE
WORTHY.

YOUR
DREAMS
ARE VALID.

MR. DEBONAIR: I need a tap teacher this weekend. Are you available to travel?
ME: Yes, sir.
MR. DEBONAIR: Good. Let's schedule a meeting for tomorrow in my office to discuss the details.

Can we please talk for a second about how magical a moment it was when Mr. Tremaine escorted me to my very first dance convention class? I just about fell to my knees in gratitude when the ballroom door opened and I spotted hundreds of joyful dancers wearing tap shoes. I'd never seen anything like it. Mr. Tremaine introduced me, and I stepped onto that huge stage and did my thing. There were no *DRAWBACKS* to the weekend, and I was *OVER THE TOP* happy. No one put a *CRAMP* in my *ROLL*.

I arrived home from that first convention experience in an idyllic state. A few days later, my bliss level skyrocketed when in the mail I received a 21-city contract from Joe Tremaine. What? They do this every weekend? I had no idea. Yes. Count me in.

Each time I enter a ballroom to teach a class, the euphoria I felt that day is what I still feel all these years later.

That $22 map was worth every penny. My assumption about Studio City paid off, and I found a teaching experience that's perfect for me.

The mind is powerful, my friend. Use yours to preview life's coming attractions. ✦

2. KNOW THYSELF

In order to heal others, we first need to heal ourselves.
And to heal ourselves, we need to know how to deal with ourselves.

~ *Thich Nhat Hanh*

Self-awareness is a conscious knowledge and a heightened understanding of yourself and those around you. Self-reflection is an ongoing practice and an empowering approach to knowing who you are. Like many aspects of life, self-awareness takes practice—which, fortunately for you, is something you know how to do extremely well. Improving in dance and in real life share some parallels. You practice choreography, right? So too must you practice enhancing personal techniques such as confidence, self-worth, positivity, patience, resolve, or anything else. Practice. Continued, deliberate, mindful, daily, and hour by hour practice.

I Still Can't Pronounce My Own First Name. From the beginning, I struggled academically. (I was slated to repeat first grade because I couldn't read.) What's more, I never could catch, see, hit, kick, or dodge a ball. My failures on the court, on the track, in the gym, and in the classroom were nothing compared to what happened on the playground. I was a goofball and an easy target. I spent most of recess playing on the swings alone or sitting inside a classroom to avoid getting beat up by the other kids. From first grade through twelfth grade, I attended thirteen different schools throughout Long Island—and my family never moved.

The world gave me my share of stuff to manage. But, fortunately, inside a dance studio I was free. Inside the studio, in a world of imagination and inspiration, I felt O.K. about myself, and I found a few hours of peace.

I did well enough in college to graduate and get a degree. Well, at least I thought I had. After graduation, I worked for MCI WorldCom. While exiting a meeting one day, a co-worker said to me, "You could go far in this organization if you were educated. There's no such word as *irregardless*, or *orientated*. Also, you should learn how to use spell check."

In spite of my shock, I was more grateful than enraged.

Later that same week, another colleague approached me, holding the sticky note I'd just left in her office. On it I'd written, *I stooped by. Your never at your desk.* We were work friends so she felt comfortable enough to approach me. She badgered me to tell her what was wrong with the note. I saw her expression slowly change from disappointment to subdued, subtle shock. I saw in her eyes that moment when she realized I had no idea what was incorrect.

I was a 27-year-old college graduate who could neither spell nor structure a sentence. And believe me when I tell you, I knew nothing about contractions. Also, I mumbled when I spoke and had to repeat myself fairly often. I couldn't even pronounce my own first name. (To this day, I still have difficulty, and people think I'm saying *Cory, Glory,* or *Maury.*) I was untrained, unschooled, and considered by a few to be uncouth.

After receiving such blatant and undeniable confirmation of my academic limitations, I had two choices. I could continue along the "ignorance is bliss" path, or I could take responsibility for my own learning. Rather than blaming my academic limitations on my environment, or accepting them as my fate, I asked myself, what could I accomplish if I put in a bit more effort?

We all have a few immutable traits, flaws, or natural inclinations holding us back from time to time. And not everything can be fixed. Yet we can take responsibility for changing the things about us that *can* be changed—the things we know *need* changing. I'm a big believer in playing to your strengths and forgiving some weaknesses. But, going through life making crazy, albeit innocent, blunders in an effort to sound intelligent wasn't an option for me. I simply was not going to treat myself that way.

Education is what the world imposes on us. Learning, on the other hand, is what we do for ourselves. All those popular and well-known quotes about staying curious started making sense to me. After all, part of our dancer's nature is our curiosity. We look at familiar happenings in unfamiliar ways—which is why, regardless of how often you take the same dance class, there's always something new to notice, discover, and learn.

Here's what I did to improve not only my language skills, but also my overall cynical and bitter outlook on life. I carried around a mini-dictionary. I wrote down hundreds of vocabulary words on little pieces of paper, and taped those inside the cabinet behind the mirror so that when I brushed my teeth, my hair, or my eyebrows, I studied. I memorized all those definitions and used the words often. I also watched the *MacNeil/Lehrer NewsHour* every day, and I repeated line by line each word of every broadcast. I listened to the audio files of anyone who sounded intelligent. And I devoured talks from motivational speakers. One of my favorites, Jim Rohn, is famous for saying, "Formal education will make you a living. Self-education will make you a fortune."

I stopped blaming externalities like my background, family, and circumstances for my deficiencies. As I changed, people responded to me in more positive ways and life started to improve. And when I became accountable for myself, I developed self-pride.

> EDUCATION IS WHAT THE WORLD IMPOSES ON US. LEARNING, ON THE OTHER HAND, IS WHAT WE DO FOR OURSELVES.

Self-improvement is neither a personality trait nor a gift given only to a few. It's something we all can do. It's realizing which skills you need to develop and what knowledge you need to acquire—and then training your mind to think about and explore the areas related to those skills and knowledge.

You've got the power of a PC in your pocket. That is, your mobile device serves as a vehicle to start your exploratory journey. Anything you're committed to learning can be found on it.

(*Side note:* I like acquiring new knowledge, but sometimes I learn facts I wish I didn't know. For instance, just recently, after years of hearing ads promoting her company, I Googled "Rosetta Stone" to see what she looked like. I assumed Stone was a last name. One of our neighbors, Mrs. Stone, had a lot of kids and some of them danced at our studio. You have no idea how disheartened I was to learn that Rosetta Stone was not a black woman. I'd listened to those TV and radio commercials with such pride. Who knew that Rosetta Stone is a rock discovered in Egypt in 1799 that became the key to deciphering ancient Egyptian hieroglyphs? (*Todavía practico mi español, pero no con Rosetta.*) ◆

Smarty Pants. I like to say I'm smart . . . smart enough to know that I don't know everything. I don't pretend to know what I don't know. People aren't stupid. (Well, not all of them.) And because of this, I surround myself with people who know more than I do in a particular area.

I can't do everything. When it comes to running the convention business, each person I manage has different responsibilities. I learn what I need to know to ensure that everyone can do their jobs, and then I do my best to let them work. That's how Malcolm Forbes does it. He once said, "Never hire someone who knows less than you do about what he's hired to do." My job is to hire individuals who are more educated than I am about the jobs they're hired to do. I need people who show up on time, do exactly what they say they're going to do, and get the job done right the first time.

I hire dancers who are at the top of their game—those who are the best at what they do and who can help me produce Tremaine Dance Conventions. With my admin staff, teaching faculty, payroll company, digital capture groups, legal teams, merchandise crew, and travel agents, I'm surrounded by dancers.

I manage these groups with the help of some top-level managers, each responsible for their own areas.

I don't do late, I don't do haphazard, and I don't want anyone's mediocre anything. Hey, if it's not worth doing, don't do it. And if you do it, do it right the first time or don't bother.

So, yes, I'm smart—at least in this area. ✦

CHECK YOURSELF.

It's easier to believe our own hype, justify our own actions, and retreat from our flaws. It's also easier to place blame on others and purposely walk away from our difficulties rather than admit our shortcomings. But when we do so, we miss out on the challenge or the opportunity (depending on your perspective) to power through and be our best. Having a conscious knowledge and an understanding of who you are can change your world(s).

WHAT ARE YOU THINKING?

Our nature is to habituate. We get set in patterns so that we'll stay comfortable, which allows our brains to exert less energy. Our minds are hardwired to protect us, their owners. The mind wants to defend itself from any information or perspective that's contrary to what it believes about its owner.

All this can make exercising self-awareness slightly more challenging. Such is the wiring we're born with—dancers and non-dancers alike.

Ponder what you're thinking about . . . because your thoughts lead to your actions.

HAVING A CONSCIOUS KNOWLEDGE AND AN UNDERSTANDING
OF WHO YOU ARE CAN CHANGE YOUR WORLD(S).

ThINKing Ink. When I was about 17 years old, I mentioned to my mom that I was considering getting a tattoo. As soon as the words left my mouth, Mother started her verbal beat-down and didn't let up for like an hour. Her message lives in my memory forever, and went something like this: "Of all the things in the world to think about, from art, to science, to world peace, is that the best you can do? You don't have anything more constructive to do with your time, your mind, or your money? You're sitting there thinking about a tattoo as if that's important. That's what you want? There are people in this world with real problems. Like not having enough food or water. The world needs solutions, but you're sitting there thinking about permanently marking up your body? Is that all you got?"

There were no volume control options and I had no place to run for silence. I was a captive audience. And even if I could get away, we had a no-door-slamming policy in our home.

Today I'm grateful that the crux of mother's sermon was about my mindset and not about tattoos or what other people would think of me or of my ink. Her lecture, as annoying as it was, was all about mindset. It left its mark on me … kinda, sorta like a tattoo. ✦

GETTING TO KNOW YOU.

If the longest journey is, in fact, the one within, delay not. Humbly accepting your shortcomings may not be easy, but it's part of personal growth. The more you know about yourself and what you stand for, the more you can balance obstinacy with honesty. Honesty will lead you to a clearer, better understanding of yourself. Obstinacy will lead you to having your head buried in the sand . . . and *then* what part of your body is up in the air?

Enough About *Me*. What Do *You* Think of Me? With an accepting and open mind, ask people who know you fairly well for their feedback about you. The same goes for your processing of their feedback, which you'll need to do later. Embrace what you hear. Did their comments have merit? Make it easy for the person to give you feedback by listening without defensiveness. If somebody points out a problem and you agree it's a problem, what can you do to improve upon or to change it? If you disagree, feeling that nothing's an issue, maintain openness and receptivity and keep listening, because no one is perfect or always right.

No One Is Perfect or Always Right. We all fall and make mistakes in life. That's reality. Strive for honesty and ask yourself questions like the following:

- Why did I get mad at _____ ?
- Why didn't I do what I said I was going to do?
- Why couldn't I just say, "I'm sorry"?
- Why was I so moody and anxious when _____ ?
- How can I gain a better perspective about _____ ?
- How did I contribute, positively or negatively, to a drama-filled situation?
- Why was it so difficult for me to admit that I didn't know the answer?
- Why did I check my mobile device while my friend was sharing her good news?
- What did I learn today about myself that I can use for self-improvement tomorrow?

First, Know Who You Are. Then, Present Yourself to Others. You won't be invited to all the parties, you're not going to fit in with every crowd, and not every gig is for you. The more you know about yourself, the better you can deal with these and other realities of life.

In order to reach your best, you must face yourself with honesty, fairness, and self-appreciation.

3. THE POWER OF THE MIND

Believe you can and you're halfway there.

~ Theodore Roosevelt

GREATNESS BEGINS IN YOUR MIND.

Your belief system, especially belief in yourself as being worthy and deserving, is important. When you believe in and trust yourself, you give yourself permission to be great—but not on the level of cocky, better than anyone else, or unwilling to help anyone else. If you're lacking in self-belief, research the subject and educate yourself on the nuances of how to improve in this area. Day to day, month to month, and through the decades, believe that the future can be better, and that you have the power to make it so.

Life Is Great and I Am Great in Life. I read a lot as a teenager. There wasn't much else to do in my small town of 250 people. Among the many books I read was Dr. Norman Vincent Peale's *The Power of Positive Thinking*. Its impact on me was enormous. After finishing it, I believed with 100% certainty that my dream of a dance career could and would come true. Dr. Peale wrote plenty of books, but this one is my favorite because it cultivated my faith in myself. "Positive thinking" is not some catchall buzz phrase.

Belief in myself makes me unstoppable. It gets me up in the morning and into the office at 6 a.m. Belief in myself is how I remain steadfast in my convictions—and it's what keeps me working and doing what I do. My own life is proof of what Confucius, a Chinese teacher, said: "Do what you love and you will never work a day in your life."

Even as a 12-year-old boy who grew up in the cotton fields of Louisiana, I always believed I was going to do well in life. This was still true even after my father lost his job. We went from a three-vehicle household to just one truck (which in those days meant you were poor). Regardless of my circumstances, I always saw opportunities instead of problems.

Despite the realities of my childhood, I still felt worthy and deserving of a good life. I carried myself like a success because I expected to succeed. I've discovered that when you expect the best, that's exactly what you get. And if you expect the worst, you're simply setting yourself up for tough times.

I worked hard for what I have, and you can do the same. You can succeed and do well in life. You absolutely have to believe that.

You also have to believe that life is good, and that life is exciting. If you don't see life as exciting, you're looking at it the wrong way. Repeat after me: *Life is great and I am great in life.* I live by these words.

I know nothing about your belief system or what makes you tick. I can tell you, though, that if you view yourself as a doer and an achiever, you'll most assuredly become exactly that—a doer and an achiever. By doing so, you'll create your own *joie de vivre*. That's a Cajun expression I heard growing up. It means "joy of living."

I can't tell you how to feel good about yourself or how to live. But I *can* tell you that getting up, dressing up, and showing up is a great beginning. Nobody will do the work for you. So, whatever it is you want, believe you have what it takes to make that happen. Because if you don't, nobody else will either.

Making it in the entertainment industry requires hard work and a mindset that never considers quitting. Period. Get a copy of Dr. Peale's book and prime your mind. *Laissez les bons temps rouler*—yet another expression I've heard all my life. Let the good times roll, baby! ✦

SELFIE-ESTEEM.

A very real concern for some of us is what other people are saying or thinking about us. Yet the reality is that most of us have so much going on in our lives that we tend to view the world through what directly affects us—and, for the most part, that's what we care about.

Fear of what people think about you is an unhealthy fear. So is being afraid of how you'll look or being scared of making a fool of yourself. (Compare these fears with a healthy fear, which protects you and helps you recognize what's actually dangerous.) If you're constantly worried about what everyone else thinks, you'll always be at their mercy. If you stop worrying about everyone else's opinions about what you're doing, what you're doing will become clearer.

T-shirt Maker. I once designed a T-shirt. It featured a graphic of a tap shoe, with the words *TAP IN to Your Full Potential* appearing in the middle of the design. But I was too scared to wear the shirt. I was worried that people would say (just not aloud), "Who does she think she is?" Time after time I would put it on and immediately take it off.

Finally, though, I wore the T-shirt in public. Doing so was the only way to push through the unhealthy fear. Guess what? I was shocked not only by the number of compliments I received, but also by how many people wanted to order one. I hadn't planned on getting into the T-shirt business. But, saying *yes* to every person wanting my shirt led to the creation of a business. By doing this, I learned about wholesale and retail shopping, pricing, order fulfillment, inventory management, sales taxes, and shipping options.

People make assessments of other people. It's part of our nature, and you can't stop someone from forming opinions about you.

But here's something you *can* do: Find your balance between acknowledging those viewpoints and letting them affect you.

This is much easier to do if you keep the following three points in mind:

1.   It's exhausting trying to mold your life around how other people perceive you.
2.   It's impossible to please and live up to everybody's expectations.
3.   It's unreasonable to worry about what people think about you once you realize how seldom they do. ✦

WHATEVER IT IS YOU WANT, BELIEVE YOU HAVE WHAT IT TAKES TO MAKE THAT HAPPEN.

OPTIMISTS IGNITE. PESSIMISTS EXTINGUISH.

While pessimists are complaining about their 99 problems to whoever will listen, self-doubt is undermining their actions. Simultaneously, they're beating up on themselves and allowing tiny misfortunes to disrupt the big picture. In the end, some incredibly talented individuals abandon their hopes and typically accomplish far less than their potential during their lifetimes. Doubting one's own abilities is pointless.

Optimists, on the other hand, see their 99 challenges for what they are: opportunities to problem-solve. Optimists are resilient. They see setbacks as a form of useful feedback and remain willing to try again. Optimists look for positive life fuel to stay powered up—not down or mediocre.

Optimism Is Your Power Resource. No one gets through life untested. Practice optimism as a way to recover from and cope with whatever the day may bring. Optimism helps you to accept the reality of a situation and focus more on the positive than the negative aspects of whatever just happened.

A NEGATIVE MINDSET OBLITERATES HOPE, IS A MASSIVE BARRIER TO ANYTHING GOOD, AND DELIVERS THE KIND OF RESULTS YOU DON'T WANT.

ENVY AND JEALOUSY: A BARRIER TO ANYTHING GOOD.

"The Soul of the World is nourished by people's happiness. And also by unhappiness, envy, and jealousy. To realize one's Personal Legend is a person's only real obligation. All things are one." So wrote Paulo Coelho.

Some people use the words *envy* and *jealousy* interchangeably, but they're different. Envy is a desire to have something that's been awarded to or achieved by someone else. "Envy is the ulcer of the soul," said the ancient Greek philosopher Socrates.

FORGET NOTIONS ABOUT "IF I HAD WHAT THEY HAVE, THEN I'D BE GOOD." YOU'RE ALREADY GOOD.

ENVY

"I want what you have." • **"I resent you for having what you have."** • **"I don't want you to have that."**

You may feel envy when your best friend arrives at dance class wearing a head-to-toe outfit you've been eyeing.

Jealousy, on the other hand, is the resentment people feel when they think someone else has something they believe should be theirs—for instance, when friends manage to book the tour and they don't.

JEALOUSY

• **"He got the part I'd have been perfect for. Now I'm worried he's trying to take over my spot."** •

• **"I put in the extra work and he didn't."** •

• **"Back off. Move out of my way. That role should have been mine."** •

No One Can Keep Your Good From You. Growing up as the dance studio owner's daughter, I learned a host of fundamental life principles. An important one was this: *There's enough for everyone.* Whenever a new studio opened close to ours, my mom's response was always the same: "There are enough students to go around." If parents were late picking up their kids at the end of the day, those kids went home with us just in time for dinner. When I expressed concern about having enough food to go around, she'd casually reply, "There's plenty for everyone." Whenever one of my teammates at my mom's studio flourished, his or her progress didn't translate as a loss for me, but a win. One dancer's success contributed toward increasing the collective average. That is, the strength of our group increased with the achievement of a teammate.

I carry these ideas about enough-ness with me today. I apply the concepts to managing tough emotions like jealousy, envy, or a combo of the two. These unpleasant feelings are reactions to ideas centered around lack and limitation. Believe in the infinite supply of good and keep the destructive green-eyed monster at bay. ✦

TAKE STOCK.

No matter how strong, rich, beautiful, smart, talented, or lovable you are, someone else can upstage you. Human nature may dictate that emotions like envy and jealousy exist, but you have the power to keep them in check. Your mindset is neither fixed nor unchangeable. You have the ability and you have the capacity to make daily and even hourly decisions to move from feeling powerless to powerful, and from feeling beaten to blessed. Take stock, and water what you've got.

Smile. You Have What You Need. In the house where I grew up with only a mom in charge, none of us kids were allowed to borrow anything from anyone. When it came to hair products, clothes, school supplies, nail polish, or cold hard cash, the slogan in our house was "If you don't have it, make do, or do without." This mantra of self-sufficiency was a lesson in reality, since in reality what we want doesn't magically come to us.

The idea of doing without until we could buy or earn what we wanted was a concept I hated as a kid. Today I realize that no matter how wealthy you are, when you appreciate what you have, you tend to have more of what you need. When something belongs to you and you've earned it, you tend to invest in and take better care of it. Smile if you're with me on this. ✦

SAY, WHAT'S THAT UP AHEAD?

Your view of what you see when you look at the world is reflected back to you. Those who see the world as dark, dank, and overwrought with pain and despair, get that back.

When you see it as exciting, challenging, and loving, the world will prove these qualities to you. The world is your mirror so use your mental floss to get a good view. This means occasionally bypassing the negativity and sensationalism we're bombarded with.

Go for what you want. See yourself where you want to be and speak affirmatively about what's possible for you. By nature, you own your ideal and have within you the power to bring your vision of yourself to fruition.

SECTION 2
DANCE EDUCATION

4. THE SPLENDORS OF DANCE

*Dance is for everybody. I believe that the dance came from the people
and that it should always be delivered back to the people.*

~ Alvin Ailey

It's probably safe to say that dance has functioned as a form of enjoyment long before any recorded history. In all likelihood, we humans danced before there was even a word for it. Little evidence is available to pinpoint the exact period when dance became a part of human culture, although paintings and literature show that it's been part of people's lives from as early as the medieval period. (Dance manuals from the Renaissance, the historical era that followed the medieval period, have survived to this day.)

EVERYBODY DANCE NOW.

Dance has been and always will be a great way for people of all ages, body types, levels of technical prowess, and with or without special needs or disabilities to creatively self-express.

Why Dance? For all sorts of reasons. In some cultures people dance to mourn, celebrate, give thanks, and express traditions. In other cultures, dance is a way to tell stories, preserve history, honor legends, or pass on social and religious norms to the next generation. Some people dance to exercise, offer healing, bond socially, or form communal ties. And still others dance to provoke or entertain audiences.

Whether it's a line dance at a school reunion, the hora at a bat mitzvah, a dance duet featuring siblings, a teary-eyed father-daughter waltz at a wedding, or a dance studio recital, dance is splendidness.

Dancers Are Smart. I've been around a long time, and I know a thing or two about working with dancers. I'm not surprised when I read studies about professionals in various fields preferring to work with and employ dancers. I know *I* do. Dancers are smart, good listeners, and fast learners. We accept instruction, visual or otherwise, well and that's because we come by it naturally. We stand alert and ready for just about anything during a dance class. And then there's what's called "musical intelligence." This is all about how listening to music increases concentration and reduces stress. Hello! Music is at the heart of what we do. Music is the reason I dance. That's the truth. Plain and simple. ◆

THE WORD IS.

The American Dance Therapy Association, American College of Sports Medicine, *New England Journal of Medicine,* Education Commission of the States, Stanford University, Carnegie Foundation for the Advancement of Teaching, and countless other organizations have conducted study after study on the effects that dance has on the mind and body. The study results have contributed to the growing evidence confirming that dance can help improve your overall health. The physical, psychological, emotional, spiritual, and social benefits are well documented.

The Elderly. In 2003, researchers at Albert Einstein College of Medicine investigated the effects that leisure activities had on the risk of dementia in the elderly. The findings of the study appeared in the *New England Journal of Medicine*: Out of 11 types of physical activities, including cycling, golf, swimming, and tennis, only one of them lowered participants' risk of dementia. That activity was (you guessed it) dance (1).

The Kids. Proof abounds that involvement in the arts, including dance, plays a critical role in academic performance. There's a positive link between children's physical activity and their academic performance in school: Children who are more active perform better. The exertion and creative thinking involved in physical activity work to reduce children's stress and excess energy, which in turn helps them to concentrate and make better decisions in academic settings.

An article titled "10 Salient Studies on the Arts in Education" appeared on the website of the Center for Online Education. Findings from these studies show that schoolchildren exposed to drama, music, and dance are more proficient at reading, writing, and math. For some kids, mixing, mingling, and connecting through dance reduce social anxiety and help to develop trust and cooperation skills (2). In "Arts Education Makes a Difference in Missouri Schools" in 2010, it was found that arts education not only improved academic achievement but also greatly improved social skills and the social success of students (3). In another study, "Neuroeducation: Learning, Arts, and the Brain," researchers showed that sustained arts education is an essential part of social and intellectual development (4).

The Music. When we hear music, our bodies are naturally predisposed to move. A powerful beat puts a tingle in your feet and makes your heart leap. Even infants are compelled to spontaneously respond to tempos and beats. John Krakauer, a Columbia University neuroscientist, stated in a 2008 *Scientific American* article that dance was a "pleasure double play." Music stimulates the brain's reward centers, while dance activates its sensory and motor circuits (5).

Your Mood. Dance activates your pleasure circuits, and as that happens your serotonin levels increase. When you're dancing, you feel great. Why? Because all the positive effects from the repetitive movements involved in dancing improve blood flow to the brain and leave you feeling fab.

Your Health. Dance can prevent many health-related harms. According to the American Cancer Society, physical activity may reduce the risk of several types of cancers, including breast and colon (6).

QUALITY OF LIFE.

Berkeley Wellness is an information letter created by the University of California's School of Public Health. A study on dance was featured in one of its issues. The participants in the study had chronic heart failure. Some of them went into a dance program of waltzing, while the others went into a moderate aerobic exercise program. The study found that dancing improved participants' heart function—and their overall quality of life—as much as the exercise program did (7).

Your Brain on Dance. In her article "5 Things That Will Happen to Your Brain When You Dance," Rebecca Beris offers scientific proof that dance is good for keeping us mentally sharp—even as we get older (8). How can something that's so fun accomplish this?

Dancing requires a dancer to make speedy decisions, and decision making is an important part of intelligence. A dancer has to visualize movements, which helps to create more neural pathways. This creation of additional pathways results in improved "muscle memory."

DANCING DOES YOU RIGHT.

It gives you more of the stuff you want:

- A happy heart
- Confidence and a sense of well-being
- A pleasant disposition
- Balance, coordination, and flexibility
- Endurance, strength, and stamina

and less of the stuff you don't want:

- Slumped-over posture
- Stress, tension, and anxiety
- A heavy heart

Dancers Are Special. This was the tag line at my family-owned and -operated dance studio. I heard these words at the studio and at home. One of my older sisters is *over-the-top* dramatic. Like captivating, make-a-splash, you-know-she's-in-the-room, can't-reel-her-in, dramatic. Whenever she communicated our tag line, you believed her. When I was a student in her class, she'd have us exit the room then require us to immediately walk back in. The second time, however, we were to make eye contact with her, our teacher; nonverbally obtain permission to enter; walk around, not through, dancers; and do so with our chin up and shoulders down... sometimes while balancing a book on our head.

My sister also held discussions on the nobility of dance, which served to place every student on notice that we had a responsibility to present ourselves well.

The hard work, sweat, and sense of accomplishment we experience on the dance floor, taken as a whole, is what gives us confidence when we're out in the real world. It's what makes us dancers know that we're special. ✦

DANCING. IT **UNRAVELS** YOUR MIND, **UNCHAINS** YOUR LIFE, **UNBINDS** YOUR EMOTIONS, AND **UNLOCKS** YOUR SOUL.

5. THE RIGHT DANCE STUDIO

You have to do the research. If you don't know about something,
then you ask the right people who do.

~ Spike Lee

The information in this chapter is useful for a parent enrolling a child in dance for the first time, for a high school student trying to make sure he or she is at the right studio for reaching future goals, or for anyone looking to start or further dance training as a young adult.

There are multiple variables involved in finding the school that feels like a good match for you. From big city schools to those in small towns, many students remain at the same dance studio for several years. Some of them spend so much time there that they refer to it as their "home away from home" and the people in it as their "second family." To gain a sense of the type of experience you'll have at a particular school, a bit of due diligence is in order.

THE VISIT.

Each school has its own vibe, tone, or energy. The studio where your friends, neighbors, or friends' children dance may not be the right place for *you*. Visit prospective schools. The presence of a knowledgeable and friendly front-desk person is a positive first sign. An administrator who greets visitors and manages customer service, scheduling, enrollment, and costume queries is ideal. If a free trial class is offered, or if there's an open house event, check it out. Do what you can to access a future student's overall experience. Check out codes of dress and conduct, teaching styles inside the classroom, organization of schedules and on-time classes, student engagement, class sizes, assistant teachers (if any are present)—and, oh, yes... be sure to check the restroom for cleanliness.

The State of the Place. A studio doesn't need to be a state-of-the-art facility. But, at a minimum, look for the following:
*   Classroom mirrors
*   Reasonable audio and other technology systems
*   Sufficient dressing room space
*   Suitable heating and air conditioning
*   Necessary safety equipment for tumbling, acrobatics, aerial, or silks classes
*   Proper flooring. Dance surfaces need to have spring, or cushioning. Flooring without sufficient "give" sends shockwaves through the body from the impact of the feet striking the floor. Concrete and other unforgiving surfaces compound the force moving through the body. Improper flooring—flooring that doesn't absorb shocks—will put undue stress on muscles, ligaments, joints, tendons, and bones. It can lead to chronic pain and injury that may last a lifetime.

All That Glitters... Some competitions liberally award prizes that don't necessarily reflect high-quality dance instruction or technical proficiency. A plethora of plaques, awards, and trophies on display at a studio should *not* weigh heavily in your en-rollment decision. It's true. All that glitters is not gold.

Where the Boys Are. Women train male dancers very effectively. Yet, at a certain point a male perspective is useful. When exploring classes for boys, consider schools with a diverse faculty and/or guest instructors.

"I Can Do That." The entry barriers for opening a dance studio are low. There are no exams, certifications, or degree requirements. Nor are there governing or controlling organizations that regulate activities or set school standards. Anyone with the desire to serve as a dance educator is at liberty to do so. Yet just because anyone can, doesn't mean that anyone should.

Head of the Class. Review teacher bios to learn who's who and who's done what. Dance education degrees, certifications, trainings, company work, and Broadway, film, television, or theater experience are some of the credits to look for.

WHO'S RUNNING THE SHOW?

There are some imperceptible and elusive elements that vary from school to school. These less apparent qualities are just as important as the others mentioned above.

Each school has a moral and ethical compass that impacts students beyond dance, extending to their outlooks on life. This compass points to a school's overall philosophical tenets. A student's experience at a school correlates directly to that school's leadership.

Leaders set ethical standards and build cultures. Young people are constantly watching and observing the adults in their lives, and they look to adults for approval, recognition, and cues as to how to approach life. Through our actions, we teach kids how to maintain a level head, constructively handle anger, amicably resolve conflicts, and find peace in the midst of life's chaos and bliss.

SIT BACK, RELAX, AND ENJOY THE SHOW.

Recitals, showcases, special performances, and competitions take place year-round. Attend a performance, and try to gauge the overall performance quality, not only of the dancers onstage, but of the production itself. Look for a diversity of dance styles in the presentation, and take into account the way older teens are costumed and the types of moves they are portraying. Appropriate movement quality and presentation, along with a good technical foundation, are important. When you see the older kids dancing in ways that make you as a parent cringe, consider that a factor in making your decision to join a particular studio. Whether you call it movement quality, or age-appropriate choreography, it's your call.

BUSINESSES RISE AND FALL ON LEADERSHIP, AND ANY ORGANIZATION IS ONLY AS GOOD AS ITS LEADERS.

Quality Dance Training for All. Unqualified teachers do their students a disservice and put them at a disadvantage. When you're not properly trained, what have you got? Not much, except for maybe some injuries. Lack of proper technique and training goes hand in hand with injury. Studies show that dancers who train in ballet are less likely to suffer from injury when dancing or engaging in other activities. On the flip side, you shouldn't put dancers en pointe too early because it's dangerous for their ankles and feet. Hello! Their bones and joints aren't fully developed yet. And what about ossification of the bones? Readiness for pointe work means more than just reaching a certain age; it requires good alignment (hip-knee-ankle-foot), range of motion, core stability, and other factors that proper training and technique can produce.

A bad dance teacher can cause great harm. So, do your research. Before enrolling, gather facts about a studio and its teachers so you can make an informed decision. Play it safe. Do business with a reputable studio. ✦

EVERY STUDENT, FROM RECREATIONAL TO SPECIAL-NEEDS TO HOPEFUL PROFESSIONAL, DESERVES QUALITY DANCE EDUCATION PROVIDED BY TRAINED AND KNOWLEDGEABLE EXPERTS.

What "Version" of a Studio Works Best for You? Every dance studio operates differently and engages in different activities. In schools where the focus is on performing, students might travel the country attending dance conventions or competitions, while students at other schools are marching in local parades and performing at charity events. One school may have an overall focus on education and technique, while another may dedicate a majority of its time to rehearsing for performances. Parents at one studio may do the fundraising, while at others the parents are hosting bedazzling costume parties in preparation for an upcoming performance. Some schools host picture days, pajama days, pool party days, family fun days, and birthday parties, or have special guests for workshops and choreography classes; others may do none of these.

There are no hard and fast rules when it comes to dance studios, and there is no one factor that says a certain school is a better choice over another.

For Parents (Part 1): Have a Great Experience. After you've enrolled your kid, there's one very specific thing you can do to ensure that a great experience is shared by all: *leave*. Trust your enrollment decision and let the teachers decide who makes what team, who advances to the next level, and who's the featured soloist. Allow instructors to serve through teaching. Hovering outside the studio doorway, or watching through two-way mirrors, or peeking through the gaps in the blinds... those are all distracting. Your kid knows you're there, and your presence changes the teaching dynamic. If you do spend time in the lobby, remain mindful of loud phone calls, or allowing your other kids to run around.

Stay on top of emails and other communications. And, if you have extenuating circumstances or a concern about something, text or email rather than bringing it up between classes, when teachers are clearly busy. Respect is always in order and greatly appreciated.

Remember that studio owners work long hours and days on end to do what they do. So please make timely payments. Professional dance educators spend years acquiring skills, both as artists and as businesspeople. They haven't taken vows of poverty. ✦

For Parents (Part 2): Take It Easy. Can you believe that parents sometimes ask me, "How can I get my child to be more outgoing onstage?" They're asking *me*—the soloist who just recently stopped staring at the floor during her own performances! I don't like performing all alone on a big stage. It's lonely and scary for me. Yet put me in a group, and I'm stress-free.

Dance isn't academic, with pass-or-fail concepts, and we each enjoy and express ourselves differently. As the gatekeeper to your child's dance education experience, let children enjoy the dance their way.
Your outlook and your actions help your kids discover who they are—but just as importantly, who *you* are. When you're unhappy, there's going to be an "unhappy dancer" (an oxymoronic phrase, by the way).

Once, while I was serving on a panel responsible for selecting dancers to receive scholarships and other opportunities, I initially thought it was unfair when the panel began to eliminate students because of how their parents behaved. I remember asking, "In what world is it O.K. to penalize someone for something they have nothing to do with?" The casting director said to me, "Time is money and we have a job to do. That mom is in our way too much." ✦

DON'T START NONE, WON'T BE NONE.
Complaining begets complaining, and then drama ensues. If you have a concern, please discuss it only with the people who have the power to fix it. Any other conversation is gossip. It's easy to find something to complain about. Bide your time, because what may seem important today may not be tomorrow. Some issues de-escalate on their own. Please keep it positive.

HAPPY PEOPLE WELCOMED AT THE DANCE STUDIO. COMPLAINERS? NOT SO MUCH.

6. IF YOU'RE LUCKY, YOU ATTEND DANCE CONVENTIONS

Dance training is life training.

~ Joe Tremaine

A dance convention is a life-changing weekend. It consists of a faculty of professional dance teachers (many having traveled from other cities) who give classes to participants according to age or ability. Many dance teachers take their students to conventions to foster growth, broaden their perspectives, and develop their artistry. You may attend a dance convention as part of a competition team, or with your dance studio, or as an independent student.

Every convention has a different feel and focus, but the formats are similar. The classes offered include a wide variety of genres, such as ballet, jazz, break dancing, musical theater, hip-hop, tap, strength and conditioning, street, partnering, ladies' heels, improvisation—even etiquette class!

A GREAT CONVENTION EXPERIENCE.

You won't find any rulebook on attending a dance convention, yet what you learned in kindergarten is enough guidance: Share, play nice with the other kids, and have fun! Whether you're a first-timer or a seasoned participant, make the most of your experience by considering some basic guidelines.

Prepare Yourself. In many areas of life, preparation is an important part of being successful. Attending a dance convention is no exception. Convention days are long, so stock your bag with all your dance shoes, extra socks, knee pads, water, healthy snacks, a mini first-aid kit, clothing changes, and deodorant, if you know you need it. Also, prepare your body with good nutrition and a proper night's rest.

Step in Time. When you're "on time," consider yourself late. Arrive 10 to 15 minutes early so that the classes, auditions, and competition can start on time. If you do join in late, do so without distracting others or disturbing the flow that's already in progress. Catch up on your own without asking someone next to you for instruction. The only conversations taking place during classes should be initiated by the instructors.

Sit or Dance. Skipping a class and missing out on an opportunity to learn something new because you're shy or intimidated doesn't make sense. If you're ill or injured, sit on the sidelines and discover how much you can learn just by watching. The operative word is *sit.* Executing cartwheels or rehearsing your own choreography in the back of the room would reflect poorly on both you, the dancer, and on your studio owner or teacher. Learn something new. Go all in and go all out.

The Other Class. An audition may be offered as part of the convention experience. If you find yourself getting anxious over the audition, simply view it as another class. Take it as an opportunity to learn new choreography or to connect with faculty teachers. Many convention auditions resemble the real-world audition process. If you're considering a professional dance career, convention auditions serve as excellent practice. At these auditions, finalists may receive scholarships to future conventions, tuition-free access to world-renowned dance schools, or other rewards. If you're dismissed before the end of the audition, observe the rest of it to understand the whole process and to determine how you can improve before your next one.

Gratitude. Throughout the convention, make eye contact with and thank the instructors after each class. Even if you have to walk from one end of a huge ballroom to the other to do so, the time and effort are definitely worth it. Expressing appreciation spreads the love.

Beyond the Convention. Make the most of what you've learned. Apply the technical corrections at your studio, and the life lessons in your daily activities.

Dancing Beyond What You Know. One of my absolutely favorite convention moments happened when I observed guest teacher Nakul Dev Mahajan teach Bollywood at our 2015 Nationals in Orlando. He was invited to teach just for that event. When I told him to expect about 400 students per class, he looked surprised. His normal class size was more like 40.

Moments before his class, I offered him a few pointers and last-minute assurances. Then I left the room, knowing that my presence might make him more nervous than he already was. I came back 45 minutes later and could not believe the transformation. Students who had never before experienced Bollywood were full out, smiling, and having the time of their lives.

That class was something to behold, and the energy was incredible. Even parents, teachers, and other observers were standing on their chairs cheering, enjoying the dancers enjoying themselves. Nakul was on fire, and he set that room on fire. I feel sorry for any dancers who skipped out because they didn't think Bollywood was something they'd ever need to learn. They missed out big time. ◆

> THAT CLASS WAS SOMETHING TO BEHOLD, AND THE ENERGY WAS INCREDIBLE.

LIBERTY TOUR.

It's not every weekend that you're exposed to so many different dance styles, working industry professionals, and dancers from other parts of the country or the world. The energy that emanates from and among the hundreds of dancers is captivating and memorable. If you've never attended a dance convention, register for one coming to your neck of the woods, pack your bag, get ready for liberation and the time of your life, and... hit the road, Jack!

7. SIGN ME UP FOR COMPETITIONS... OR NOT

If you can dance and be free and not embarrassed, you can rule the world.

~ Amy Poehler

At a dance competition, groups of all sizes compete in a variety of styles while a professional panel of judges offer improvement tips and critiques.

Winning is great—there's no doubt about it, but the ultimate success relates to the lessons learned, not just to the final scores. Transferable life skills like leadership, camaraderie, good sportsmanship, and accountability are by far the more valuable prizes.

While some dancers thrive on it, competition isn't for everyone. Some dancers prefer performing not for a prize, but for the sheer joy of dancing. That's cool.

Performing Live Is Cause For Celebration. I've had my share of bungled performances, and I've learned from them. Perhaps my first one took place when I was eight years old, while dancing in a military tap number. I'd noticed that my bow tie was vertical rather than horizontal. During a quick costume change my mother had put it on me in a rush. I spent the entire number tap dancing away while also trying to adjust the bow tie. Thanks, Mom!

Of course, after years of experience, I now know that ignoring the bow tie would have allowed me to focus on my performance. Audiences don't care about the mishaps—it's how you handle yourself during and in response to those mishaps that matters.

Dancers need to learn what it means to perform onstage, and dance competitions are an excellent opportunity to practice. If you have the honor and privilege of being involved in a competition and performing onstage, consider yourself one of the luckiest people in the world.

Celebrate the performance, not the win. Life involves trade-offs and compromises. No one walks away a winner all the time. You can't win until you learn what it is to lose, and it's how you react to losing that shows the world who you are.

Finally, the stage is sacred space. Performing on one is an honor. If you're fortunate enough to dance and perform, you've been given a real gift. Thank your parents and your dance teachers.

The rest of what I have to say is directed to parents and teachers.

I get annoyed when I hear about how one adult ruined a competition experience for an individual dancer, or for an entire group, by pushing for wins, by meting out punishment for mistakes, or by bad-mouthing a dancer. All this negativity robs performers of their joy for dance. Whether your kids and students win or lose, tell them, "I'm proud of you for getting out there and doing your thing." No more, no less. Winning is indeed wonderful. But the performance—not a prize or trophy—is what really matters. You can be disappointed in the results yet still celebrate the dancers' performance.

Adults who teach kids to congratulate and cheer on other dancers are my kind of people. It's about kindness. Even backstage etiquette counts. It may not help with someone's onstage performance score, but good sportsmanship speaks volumes. ✦

A NOTE TO AUDIENCE MEMBERS.

While performers are onstage, they put forth their best efforts—and they ask that you do the same as members of the audience by showing these common courtesies.

Remain seated, and limit entering and exiting the hall while dancers are performing. If you absolutely must move about, do so only during the applause at the end of a performance.

Keep electronic distractions to a minimum.

Hooting and hollering at a sporting event makes sense, but not at a dance arts performance. Such actions not only annoy and disturb other audience members, they can also potentially diminish the quality of the experience for the entire house—performers included.

Model positivity and kindness by applauding everyone, regardless of whether you know them.

Hold your final applause during and just after those few magical ending moments of a performance, while the last chord of the music still hangs powerfully in the air. There's something to be said about those few seconds of silence that follow the conclusion.

8. TRAINING THROUGH THE YEARS

The purpose of training is to tighten up the slack,
toughen the body, and polish the spirit.

~ Morihei Ueshiba

Whatever you're looking for, whether it's to jump-start your career, acquire job experience, gain exposure to the professional world of dance, earn a degree, attain certification, enhance your technique, perform, travel, or network with top-notch, esteemed professionals, it is likely you can find what you're looking for.

An array of training tracks and platforms in anything from music to drama to other art-related fields, including hip-hop, tap, ballet, and beyond, are on the rise. World-class dance companies, academies, fine art institutes, colleges of dramatic arts, and major commercial dance studios offer technical and artistic training options for kids as young as 8. Some are highly competitive, others... not so much.

While the offerings vary, they are alike in that they are — drumroll, please —

INVESTMENTS IN YOUR PERSONAL GROWTH.

Charter Schools. Charter schools are start-ups created by parents, teachers, community organizations, or individuals interested in establishing additional educational prospects for kids. Charter schools typically focus on technology and the arts, are open to all, do not charge tuition, offer flexible home-school options, and are convenient for dancers attending full-time dance programs. Students opting for online courses can choose self-paced options, to work on as their own schedules permit, or can log on at certain times for virtual classes.

Performing Arts Schools. If you're looking to express yourself in a creative environment, surrounded by like-minded students and teachers who value the arts with the same passion and respect that you do, consider a performing arts school. Your chance of finding such a middle or high school near you continues to improve as these schools become more popular. They exist across the country—from Hollywood, San Diego, and Las Vegas to points east including Dallas, Detroit, Pittsburgh, Washington D.C., and West Palm Beach.

Summer Intensives. If there's something specific you want to learn or accomplish during the summer, these in-depth, short and sweet, mini-conservatory-like experiences may be right for you. Some of these development workshops, festivals, and camps require auditions, while others have open registration.

Internships. Enhance your production knowledge and gain hands-on, behind-the-scenes experience in areas such as production, program management, marketing, fundraising, technical theater, education, and operations. Interning is a way to explore the fundamentals while gaining an inside look at a specific field of study, a company, or an individual.

Studio Development Programs. Studio scholarship or apprenticeship programs are for aspiring professional dancers who want to break into the industry. They may last from 4 months to 2 years, depending on the coursework. Whether you're a college grad or a recent high school grad, these programs offer pragmatic classes and comprehensive development to further sharpen your skills. You get to train and network with influential industry pros and perform in studio showcases.

Full Immersion. Immersion programs are unique, concentrated classes or experiences associated with schools and organizations. They may take place before school, after school, or as part of the regular daily curriculum. They differ in scope and in how they're offered: through an elementary school, local community center, college, or world-famous professional dance studio.

Conservatories. A conservatory is a highly focused arts school that offers intense training in disciplines such as music, theater, and dance. The major portion of study is usually in a particular art form rather than general academia. That is, conservatories don't offer a lot of academic classes because they typically focus on art forms.

Company Programs. If there's a company you've always wanted to work with, consider auditioning for a position as an apprentice, trainee, or second-company member. If you're between the ages of 16 and 23, you can test-run a professional dance company and experience the excitement of rehearsing and performing alongside its members before actually becoming a member. Imagine fine-tuning your skills and getting a feel for a particular company, while simultaneously gaining perspective into the professional life of a dancer, in a structured and educational environment.

And, there are company programs within your favorite dance conventions. In these, you travel, assist faculty teachers during their classes, and dance, like literally dance, all weekend. Attend a dance convention to learn more. (See the chapter "If You're Lucky, You Attend Dance Conventions.")

College. Many colleges offer specialized arts programs for artists who want to perfect their skills and get a degree. For those interested in careers as teachers or business owners, earning a degree at a traditional college allows you to find employment at a school or start your own business.

An aspiring dance studio owner or instructor would benefit from a college degree in dance, business, and/or marketing.

Before You Go. Before pursuing training outside your dance school, talk to your studio teachers. Seek their counsel and let them assist you in decision-making, goal-setting, and maybe even a little networking. Keep the lines of communication open.

If you're fortunate enough to take advantage of additional training, but don't end up pursuing an arts career, your performing arts and enrichment experiences will have been time and money well spent. Believe you me. ✦

WHEN THE URGE TO ENGAGE IN ALL THINGS DANCE IS A CONSTANT IN YOUR LIFE,
YOU'LL LIKELY BE . . .

REGISTERING for a dance convention

ATTENDING an intensive or workshop

STRATEGIZING schedules

COORDINATING class times

ORGANIZING your dance or costume bag

REHEARSING

BOOKING airfare

PACKING your suitcase

TAKING an online course to maintain your academic acumen

STUDYING your lines

RESEARCHING colleges

SOLICITING letters of recommendation

WRITING an admission statement

PURSUING an agent... who's already heard great things about you

SCHEDULING a visit with your agent

FILMING your latest demo reel

SCRUTINIZING new headshots

SHOWING OFF your fav headshots

PLANNING a trip to the theater

PERFORMING

VISITING family and friends backstage following your encore performance

VISUALIZING choreography

COMPOSING a note of gratitude to a dance teacher

SOAKING your tired, aching feet

SECTION 3
A CAREER IN DANCE

9. DANCE AS A WAY OF LIFE

*If you're crazy enough to do what you love for a living,
then you're bound to create a life that matters.*

~ Herb Kelleher

Like many of you, our love for dance began when we were young shining stars at our local dance studios. The dance bug bit early and fast. Our passion for dance was so great that we had to find a way to build a life and career in and around it. In other words, dancing as a way of life was something we absolutely had to do. Today, we're deeply grateful.

Bitten by the Dance Bug in Oak Ridge, Louisiana. Music was my first love. And dance goes hand in hand with music.

I grew up in the South. In a town of fewer than 250 people surrounded by plantations and cotton fields. There wasn't much to do. School, church, and Bible study. That was it.

My family owned a small grocery store and a sandwich shop. I would hang out in the back rooms with my dad's African-American workers and the field hands from nearby plantations. We'd listen to music. Music is what I love, and that's what inspired me to start dance. Music is the reason I dance.

When I was five, my dear mother enrolled me in dance classes. We drove 35 miles each way, three times a week. She used some of our family's food money to pay for my classes and costumes. (She never told my father she did that, and she suggested that I not mention it to him either.) At five years of age, the dance bug bit me and I found my calling, all at the same time.

I'm happy to report that I've lived in a "5, 6, 7, 8" world ever since. ◆

Bitten by the Dance Bug in Hempstead, New York. Dance has always been a part of my life. My mother owned a studio on Long Island. I took all sorts of classes, from tap to African dance to gymnastics.

Just about the time my feet could no longer endure the pain of one more ballet class in pointe shoes, I hit puberty. My hips expanded, and that was the end of that. I've been wearing tap shoes ever since. ◆

HAVING TO MOVE TO THINK.

As a child, Dame Gillian Lynne didn't perform well in school. Administrators referred to her as hopeless and suggested she might have a learning disorder. Gillian's mother took her to a doctor and told him about Gillian's endless fidgeting and overall lack of focus. After listening closely to her mother and carrying out a thorough physical exam on Gillian, the doctor told the girl he needed to talk to her mother privately. He turned on the radio and walked out. Then he had Gillian's mother watch her daughter through a two-way mirror. Gillian was dancing to the music. The doctor turned to Gillian's mother and said something like, "Your child isn't ill. She's a dancer. Take her to a dance school."

When Gillian arrived at the dance school for the first time, she discovered a whole new world. She has said that she walked into the room and "it was full of people like me. People who couldn't sit still. People who had to move to think" (1).

Thanks to an insightful and patient doctor, a fidgety girl found her calling. What followed was a career spanning more than fifty years, in which Dame Gillian Lynne was a dancer, choreographer, writer, producer, and director. She was a leading soloist in the original Sadler's Wells Ballet, a star dancer at the London Palladium, and an actor in films opposite Errol Flynn. She won the Olivier Award and the "Mr. Abbott" Award. She was honored by the Royal Academy of Dance with the Queen Elizabeth II Coronation Award.

You may know of her through her groundbreaking work as the original choreographer of *Cats* and *Phantom of the Opera*. She has more than fifty Broadway, West End, and opera credits to her name, and she is credited as well with some of the most successful musical theater productions in history. She even staged, choreographed, and directed many of the famous *Muppet Show* episodes.

Dame Gillian Lynne has given pleasure to millions... all while earning millions.

How Do You Dance? Where does your urge to create come from? That's just one of the questions that appear in *Masters of Movement: Portraits of America's Great Choreographers* by Rose Eichenbaum, a dancer turned photographer, who also shot the photos for our book. In *Masters of Movement,* Daniel Ezralow wrote the following: "There is no manual, no road map to a successful dance career. You have to draw, write your own map. I'm still traveling an unmarked road with its detours and blind spots" (2).

WHAT'S YOUR DANCE STORY?

Each of us has different experiences and arrives at the profession in all sorts of ways. What about you? How has dance changed or given meaning to your life? Can you tell your story in six words?

The concept of a six-word memoir comes from the entertaining book *Not Quite What I Was Planning,* in which famous people write their memoirs in just six words. For example, Taylor Swift's is "My diary is read by everyone." Deepak Chopra's is "Danced in fields of infinite possibilities." The author Elizabeth Gilbert wrote, "Me see world. Me write stories!" Laurie's dance memoir is, "Chocolate makes me tap dance faster." Joe's ahead of the game. He's been saying, "I live in a '5, 6, 7, 8' world" since before six-word memoirs were a thing. **Post your six-word dance memoir to Twitter or Instagram using @DanceintoLife #DanceintoLife.**

HOW HAS DANCE CHANGED OR GIVEN MEANING TO YOUR LIFE?
CAN YOU TELL YOUR STORY IN SIX WORDS?

10. RELOCATION NAVIGATION

You cannot win if you're not at the table. You have to be where the action is.

~ Ben Stein

Dance is everywhere and, depending on the work you want to do, different entertainment sectors offer different opportunities. While some dancers gravitate toward New York, Los Angeles, or Las Vegas, others pursue work in Chicago, Seattle, Nashville, Atlanta, Miami, or Orlando. There are lots of viable markets for performers. Of course, wherever you go will be better simply because *you're* there.

Whether you're ready to run away with the circus, head to the five boroughs, or take on Hollywood, when you make a major life decision, forethought is essential.

....

Steps on Broadway. Having specific career objectives is the only way to take some of the guesswork out of where to relocate. Many industry jobs require travel. So, the more specific you are about what you want to do, the greater your chances of having a good relocation experience.

Forget what you may have seen or heard about a city, and don't move somewhere just to follow your friends. Do your own research and consider what's right for you. There's no excuse for being uninformed about anything these days. Information is at your fingertips.

Look for an internship or apprenticeship doing the kind of work you want to do, then get in the game and play it... full out, if you please. You can't win sitting on the sidelines, and the only way to really know what you can do is to put yourself out there and try. Try new things, and work to improve upon what did or didn't work yesterday. I live by the words *veni, vidi, vici*, which, if you're not familiar with this Latin phrase, translates as "I came, I saw, I conquered."

My best and most memorable summer was spent as an apprentice working at The Little Theatre on the Square in Sullivan, Illinois. In 2005, *USA Today* named it one of the "Top 10 Places to See the Lights Way Off Broadway." Alan Alda, star of the television show *M*A*S*H,* was my roommate. I learned a lot working with several Broadway professionals, one of whom was Margaret Hamilton, best known for her portrayal of the Wicked Witch of the West in *The Wizard of Oz*. I was still a teenager, yet I'd earned my Actors' Equity card by performing in over forty musical productions (during which I learned to sew curtains and costumes, craft props, paint scenery, maintain theater facilities, network with professional performers and, of course, perform).

Later, I traveled by Greyhound bus from New Orleans to New York City, spending two days and nights sitting upright. I was headed for the Big Apple, and that was all I knew and all I cared to know. I had $300 in my pocket.

It was 1964, and *Hello, Dolly!* was on Broadway at the St. James Theatre on 44th Street between 7th and 8th Avenues. Carol Channing had the lead, and Gower Champion was both director and choreographer. I lived at the YMCA on 34th Street in Hell's Kitchen, sharing a room, sleeping on a cot, and having to use the facilities down the hall. For me, the bus ride was like a limousine, and my living quarters were like Buckingham Palace. Every penny I earned went toward food, rent, and dance classes. While in New York, I worked through a temporary employment agency. I knew my way around a keyboard—a typewriter keyboard, that is. I could type something like 100 words per minute, and because of that and my ability to take speedwriting, I supported myself through clerical jobs. I also worked as a social worker and an assistant to a detective. I taught high school and college dance classes, I stocked grocery store shelves during the graveyard shift, and I waited tables to have money to pay for dance classes. That's all I did, every single day—go to classes, to auditions, and to work.

I was a company member of a Yiddish group specializing in Jewish dance traditions of Eastern Europe. The troupe, led by modern dancer Felix Fibich, was called The Felix Fibich Dancers. We worked with famous Borsht Belt comedians like Mickey Katz, who recorded Yiddish parodies of pop songs from the 1940s to the late 1960s for RCA Victor and Capitol Records. (Katz was like the Weird Al of his day, and he's the father of Broadway legend Joel Grey, and grandfather to *Dancing with the Stars* champion and *Dirty Dancing* actress Jennifer Grey.)

I'm versatile, and I was a pretty good tap dancer. Back when I was just getting started, I offered coaching sessions in different styles of dance to make a few extra dollars. I can still tap—I just need to wear my old tap shoes because they know all the steps. ✦

I'LL TAKE MANHATTAN.
"The City," as it's known throughout much of the eastern United States, can be tough—hence the line of that song Ol' Blue Eyes, Frank Sinatra himself, sang about being able to make it anywhere if he could make it in New York. Yet, tough or not, the Big Apple is the place to be if you love theater.

The city's subway system is the largest mass transit system in the world. Getting around is easy, and a personal car isn't necessary. With regard to living space, since apartments are generally quite small and costly, people often double or even triple up.

CALIFORNIA DREAMIN'.
Start and stop, red lights, green lights, long lines—and that's just the traffic. The audition lines are sometimes just as long. Los Angeles, the "City of Angels," is the hub of filmmaking, television, and commercials, and it's where both authors of this book reside. The climate is warm, the coastlines are beautiful... and driving only between the hours of 11 p.m. and 6 a.m. still doesn't guarantee you won't encounter traffic. Here, traffic always seems to be at its peak. And yet you can never use traffic as an excuse for lateness. Almost four million people populate Los Angeles, and yet you may still occasionally spot a celebrity.

VEGAS, BABY.
Las Vegas has been called the "Miracle in the Desert." It's a city built on entertainment and renowned for its casinos, shopping, nightlife, and a dry summer heat with highs approaching 120 degrees. Vegas is more affordable to live in than Los Angeles or New York, and its grid-like layout makes it easy to navigate by car. A monorail links major resorts, hotels, and attractions.

Large-scale productions featuring some of the music industry's biggest stars, and casino-based shows, some of which have long runs, offer steady work. There are jobs available in film, television, and music videos. Cirque du Soleil, one of the largest employers of dancers worldwide, holds residency at some casinos. Cirque employs teachers, rehearsal directors, dance captains, massage therapists, artistic directors, coaches, managers, choreographers, and artists for productions and special projects. If you're a specialty artist, such as a contortionist, stilt walker, break dancer, fire artist, or aerialist, they've probably got a job for you as well.

Lost in the Corporate Shuffle. During my corporate career, I worked 12-to14-hour days, each more miserable than the one before it. It was easy to wake up, go to work, collect a paycheck, go home feeling unfulfilled, and repeat. This cycle was even worse during my minimum wage days, when I anxiously awaited a payday just to pay the bills. Going through such an experience was how I learned that money doesn't buy goods—time does.

Like many worker bees, I wondered, "What should I do with my life?" I desperately wanted to move to Los Angeles to dance. But people whose opinions I valued told me I wasn't being realistic, that dance wasn't a suitable or viable career option. They called my dreams pure folly.

So many people with a "play it safe" mindset quizzed me using one version or another of the following: "You want to quit your job and move to LA, a place you've never been, to tap dance for a living—and you have no idea how you're going to make money? Didn't you just spend two years getting your graduate degree? Isn't that like going backwards in life and wasting your potential?" Then they'd try to placate me by saying, "Besides, you have a good-paying job, great benefits, and health insurance. You've got it all. What else could you possibly want?"

What I wanted was to enjoy some aspect of my life and to stop feeling like a coward, afraid to trust herself. I wanted to find a way to never, ever have to go back to working a day job. I was scared to quit, and even more scared about what my life would look like if I didn't. I began to ask questions like these: *Am I willing to work as hard for me as I do for this corporation? If I can work 14-hour days to make someone else wealthy, will I invest that same energy in my own development? Do I believe I can make enough to support myself even if I have to rent a room in a house or live in a studio apartment?* My answer to each question was "Yes!"

Making the statement at age six that you want to be a professional dancer is cute. Making that same statement at age 26 is different. Confirmation that it was O.K. for me to dream of a life as a tap dancer came from a therapist. She said, "Identify what you love to do and be really good at it—like, *really* good at it. Do that and don't worry about the money. The money will come."

I thought about that statement for years before finally realizing that I had nothing to lose by believing it was true. I was consumed with doubt, and my mind was riddled with negative mental chatter. Fortunately, there was a louder inner voice screaming, "Get out now. Cut your losses. Take a chance on yourself. You're not getting any younger. Just leap already!"

And that was it. I resigned. I ignored any lingering apprehension. I discounted the naysayers and filtered out the chatter enticing me to be someone I wasn't. And when my manager offered to increase my salary if I would stay, I felt empowered saying, "No, thank you."

I couldn't figure out a career goal. There was no epiphany or moment of clarity. Of the 40,000 to 70,000 thoughts we humans have daily, during that time in my life most of mine were simply *I want to earn a living as a tap dancer*. It wasn't the most specific goal, but it was all I had. So I held on to it by repeating it hour by hour and day by day, until I began to believe I could achieve it. Finally I asked, "Why not me?" Obviously it was possible, because there were lots of other people earning a living as dancers.

I knew I wasn't going to book a world tour or dance on Broadway. And I had no desire to start my own tap dance company, since I don't much care for managing people or handling logistical details. I like things simple.

> IDENTIFY WHAT YOU LOVE TO DO AND BE REALLY GOOD AT IT— LIKE, REALLY GOOD AT IT.
>
> DO THAT AND DON'T WORRY ABOUT THE MONEY.
>
> THE MONEY WILL COME.

Here's the prayer I prayed: "I want to teach tap because that's what I do best. I want to teach different people as often as possible. I want a class rate higher than I'd be paid teaching at a local studio. I want to teach few hours but make the kind of money I would make working 30 hours a week at one studio. Travel would be ideal. And the icing on the cake would be the opportunity to perform. I'd prefer to perform with other tappers, but if I must go solo, I will."

Up to this point in my life, I'd never heard of a dance convention. But, soon enough I was teaching tap dance at one of them. (See the chapter titled "What Do You Want from Life?" for more details on this story.)

Our minds are powerful. Think deeply about what you want and then enthusiastically declare that you're going to turn your dreams into plans. You become what you think about, and the fact that you conjured up your dream makes it yours. You own it, and you're capable and worthy of accomplishing it. Go there in the mind and you'll go there in the body.

Give no energy to doubtful thoughts. And when you have rough days or years, there's a great solution for the problem of falling off your path: You stand up and you cheer yourself on.

Success isn't some endpoint or destination. Your goals and your everyday efforts toward accomplishing them *are* the success. Your ventures and adventures are the success gifts you give yourself. Success is daily, and it's available to you through your own unique pursuit.

Make yourself available to your possibilities. Because your possibilities are your fuel. And, if you're an artist, success may have less to do with having more, and more to do with being more. Spending decades going for your brand of greatness is what's so great. The very idea of going for what you want will make you feel just a bit more accomplished and a bit more prepared for whatever could possibly pop up next in life.

There's absolutely no good reason for you or anyone else to suggest that you're incapable of going for what you want in your life. Forget what other people want for you, or what someone else's journey looks like. Forget feeling foolish or guilty about wanting what you want. Put in your time, pay your dues, and go for great. Resist turning back before you've given a fair shot at realizing anything close to your ultimate dream.

Think about where you want to go. Then work to get there. And if you suspect that someone doubts what you can accomplish, use that person's doubt as your ammunition to go for what you want.

The things we want to do the most are usually the most scary. When I'm scared, I recall this quote (which is one of my top five favs of all time): "Take the first step in faith. You don't have to see the whole staircase, just take the first step." Thank you, Martin Luther King, Jr. ◆

(See the chapter titled "What Do You Want from Life?" for more details on this story.)

OUR
MINDS
ARE
POWERFUL.

AND, IF YOU'RE AN ARTIST, SUCCESS MAY HAVE LESS TO DO WITH HAVING MORE, AND MORE TO DO WITH BEING MORE.

DON'T TRIP.
Resist losing your way by letting yourself become inundated by distractions with friends, partying, or socializing. Keep in mind your primary reason for relocating, then stick with a self-discipline game plan to ensure that you always return to the work at hand: remaining positive and building a life around what you love.

11. AUDITIONING

We keep going back, stronger, not weaker, because we will not allow rejection to beat us down.
It will only strengthen our resolve. To be successful there is no other way.

~ Earl G. Graves

An audition is an evaluation of your artistic skills. It's your opportunity to express your artistry and to share what makes you special. It's one of the paths to finding work in the entertainment industry. While there's no magic formula or hidden trick for booking jobs, there are steps you can take to ensure that you enter the room with a calm, cool, and collected certainty.

YOU CAN'T NAIL AN AUDITION ON HOPE.

Anyone who tries out for *A Chorus Line* yet is completely unfamiliar with the iconic choreography for "I Hope I Get It" not only won't get the job, but doesn't deserve it. Prepare for the great experience of an audition, and learn as much as you can about the job being cast. Research footage, websites, and social postings with the objective of gathering information about the hiring companies or individuals.

Maintaining physical aptness is another facet of preparation. How you take care of yourself is part of your credibility.

Style Sheet. If you know that a show is casting for a specific look or character, play the part. Go edgy or wear the superhero costume. Maintain a tasteful aesthetic, and use the following as your ultimate guiding principle: *When in doubt, don't.*

Don't go so far as to show up to audition for Dorothy in *The Wizard of Oz* in a blue dress and two long braids, because that may not go over well. Idina Menzel, when auditioning for *Wicked*, wore green eye makeup. She didn't do a full face of color, but hinted at it with eye shadow and eyeliner.

For *Mamma Mia,* cut-off shorts, wavy hair, and full-flow Mediterranean patterns demonstrate that you're familiar with the material and are able to showcase the knowledge you have by *hinting* at the show's qualities.

Make it easy for casting people to picture you in a certain role. If you don't look the part, then show up as the best version of you.

The Kitchen Sink. Bring a variety of dance shoes and backup outfits so you can change if you find that your look is off the mark. Bring extra résumés, headshots, and business cards. Pack deodorant, a towel, water, plastic bags for wet clothes, and healthy snacks.

STRUT YOUR STRENGTHS.

Dance expresses who you are without using words, and your wardrobe does the same. Let your authentic style and vibe show through by choosing apparel that accentuates your lines, flatters your physique, and allows you to own the floor and dance like nobody's watching.

But remember to cover what needs covering because, in fact, people *are* watching. We like what Epictetus said: "Know, first, who you are, and then adorn yourself accordingly."

You've Got the Look. Dance plays no favorites, but typecasting does. It dictates specific traits, physical or otherwise. Casting agents want to determine your aptness to serve in a particular role. If you don't have a particular physique or personality, then that's that. If casting is looking for 5'7" and taller, a specific age range, an ethnicity, or a character resemblance, you may walk into an audition and get cut before hello. They don't need you today because you *don't* have the look.

As you make your exit, smile and express gratitude for the experience... and be nice to the person holding the clipboard or tablet.

Chin Up. Posture and body language shape not only how people see you, but how you feel about yourself as well. As Martha Graham reminds us, "Stand up! Keep your backs straight! Remember that this is where the wings grow."

The Eyes Have It. During the audition, focus on what *you're* doing and why *you're* in the room. Use the mirror to gaze into your own eyes. Resist judging your success or progress based on someone other than yourself.

Fix You. Directors and choreographers, in addition to offering approval and accolades, offer critiques and corrections. You're not there to receive coddling. If someone acknowledged you and took the time to tell you how to improve, look them in the eye for a few seconds, apply the correction, and say, "Thank you." (Studies have shown that holding someone's gaze helps that person recall you more easily.)

Put aside your feelings, because doing your best is more important than how you feel at that moment. If a comment is delivered more harshly than you would like it to be, it's not personal. It's business... show business.

The Fall. Directors and choreographers don't expect perfection. As a matter of fact, dancers who fall flat on their faces *still* get callbacks. That's because they were living and giving their all just prior to the misstep. Stay calm. Your recovery, more than any blip, slip, trip, or dip, exposes your ability to think on your feet. If you fall, make it part of the dance.

Next! Regardless of your talent, you're likely to experience what you may call rejection. It's not. It's a *no* for today. That's it and that's life.

In 1980, Paula Abdul auditioned for the Los Angeles Laker Girls with 700 other women. After her first-round cut, she registered again, this time wearing a different outfit. She changed both her hairstyle and the spelling of her name. She was cut again. She told her friends, who were also cut and ready to leave, that she wasn't going with them because she had one more outfit.

On the third round, when groups were told to switch lines from front to back, she held her position in the front and was finally chosen. Of course, what worked in the 1980s won't work today because of wristbands and other check-in and check-out procedures. But here's the takeaway: A fixed mindset, under the right circumstances, is a good thing.

"I'm used to not being selected. I'm used to rejection, which I embrace because I have nothing to lose," Abdul has said (1). Her dance training, which she credits to Joe Tremaine, opened the door to her career, and she did the rest. She established herself as a singer, songwriter, choreographer, actress, and television personality.

An Invitation to Return. A callback translates to "Show me again why I liked you the first time." Whatever you did during round one worked. Help the directors remember you and what they liked about you by not changing too much in your appearance, unless you're otherwise instructed. A callback may take place on the same day as the initial audition, or your agent may notify you about a future date and time. It depends on the gig.

You may have several callbacks and perform the combination you previously learned, or you may learn a new combo. Some callbacks are for different styles. Others are for partnering work—that is, to pair groups of performers and determine who matches best with whom.

TAKE NOTE.

Keep an audition log book, or use an app like Evernote to write down what each audition was for and what you did. Here's an example: *Did short jazz-type combo. Asked to stay and tap. Did basic time steps and over the tops. Sang "Twinkle, Twinkle, Little Star" when asked for 16 bars.*

Just as important, take note of who was in the room. You're auditioning, and at the same time you're building relationships. If you go to an audition with the same casting director who saw you at a previous audition, it makes a huge difference if you reference the other time you've been in front of that director. But do this only if you have the opportunity to make light conversation.

Also, after you've worked with a director, look to see if his or her name is attached to a new project. Then, when you're auditioning for that theater, or company, or show, you can say you've worked with the director they're using. This becomes a point of reference, should one casting agent decide to ask that director if you're a valuable hire.

Embrace Your Inner Singer. There are dancers who act, actors who sing, singers who dance, and then there are those exceptionally diverse artists who can execute all three. You don't need to be an opera singer, but if singing is part of a gig, get comfortable enough to croon at least 16 bars of material... yes, in front of people. You'll make a great impression if you bring the sheet music to a couple of songs, perhaps a standard and a ballad.

Today, more theater and concert work requires artists who are triple-threat, and writers, directors, and choreographers prefer hiring people who can do all three. It was 1964 when I moved to New York City. In those days, lead actors often exited the stage during big production numbers, leaving us dancers to execute the choreography. Now things are different.

A triple-threat legend and my dearest friend, Chita Rivera, is regarded as a national treasure and one of Broadway's most accomplished and versatile performers. Chita has worked to earn her status through endurance, grit, tenacity, and maybe, just maybe, a bit of gene pool luck. Chita's got the whole package: pizzazz, allure, and magnetism—all of which have made her a crowd favorite for over six decades.

Jennifer Lopez started out dancing in stage musicals and music videos, and today she's a megastar and mega-entrepreneur.

Rita Moreno's showbiz career has spanned over 70 years and counting. She's one of the few EGOT names in the industry, meaning she has won all four major annual American entertainment awards: Emmy, Grammy, Oscar, and Tony.

Develop your versatility. If coaching or classes aren't something you can afford to do right now, get involved in your school, church, clubs, community theater, or faith-based organizations to practice your skills. When you can, take acting and musical theater classes so you can learn stage techniques, develop characters, and improve the quality of your voice. You want to get comfortable enough to read sides and scripts, should you be given the opportunity. ✦

New Direction. My very first LA audition began with jazz, which is bad news for someone who dances from the ankles down. I'm certain it was my port de bras that gave me away.

Since I don't bevel, glam, pirouette, strut, or point my toes, it was obvious to me that queuing up with hundreds of commercial dancers for an audition wasn't a sound strategy. It made no sense for me to continue along this path. When I moved to LA, my goal was to dance. I promised myself I'd never use my degrees as a means to get a non-dance-related job. Non-dance work makes me want to cry. It doesn't feed me the way dance does.

I printed business cards and headed to a place on the map called Studio City. I went there in search of a way to support myself and to do what I do best: teach tap. ✦

Where's the Next Audition? I've had my fair share of failed quests, and whether they happened at an audition, onstage, backstage, or anywhere else, I never saw them as failures. I pay attention to the lesson and what to do or not do the next time.

I refuse to sit around reliving what didn't go as planned. I take a few minutes, bang my head against the wall, get myself together, and say, *Onward and upward—the show must go on.*

You're not always going to achieve perfection. So, coping with disappointment is something you have to figure out how to do—and only *you* know what works for your temperament and disposition.

I once had a roommate who, after being cut from an audition, pouted on the sofa for days. When I could no longer stand his woe-is-me whining, I shouted, "Move on already. Let it go. It's over. What's the point in rehashing what you can't change? And stop asking me what went wrong or why they didn't select you. How should I know? I'll tell you what I do know. You need to get up off that sofa and ask yourself one question and one question only: *Where's the next audition?*" ✦

TO QUOTE ONE EXPERT OF FUN, DR. SEUSS: "TODAY IS GONE. TODAY WAS FUN. TOMORROW IS ANOTHER ONE."

QUE SERA, SERA.

When it's over, let go of what you did, did not do, or wish you had done. Over-thinking or rehashing what transpired is of little value, especially considering that the next move isn't yours to make.

The outcome of an audition doesn't define you. Take your very own honest yet loving personal inventory about where you need to make improvements. Were you versatile enough to adapt to different styles when asked to do something outside the breakdown? What about your pick-up skills and your ability to quickly make corrections? Were you able to learn the choreography and interpret movements to your satisfaction? What about your strength, athleticism, endurance, and physique?

If you performed your absolute best, what more could you ask of yourself? What will be, will be.

12. REPRESENTATION

If you want to go fast, go alone. If you want to go far, go together.
~ African Proverb

Rather than host open calls and sort through hundreds or thousands of photos and résumés, many companies wanting to hire dancers save time and money by contacting a talent agency. Agents act as a liaison between you, their client, and casting directors, production companies, choreographers, and other industry entities. They help you get seen at auditions, submit and pitch you for jobs, and negotiate contractual agreements for you. They book work for you by matching, promoting, and representing you to potential employers.

It's possible to succeed without representation, but having the right agent can make all the difference in your career.

GETTING AN AGENT.

Ideally, you'll be given a personal recommendation or reference by an established teacher, choreographer, colleague, director, or someone else who can speak to your credibility. Such a recommendation can work wonders.

Agencies scout for talent at conventions, competitions, workshops, intensives, and other industry events. Many agencies hold open calls once or twice a year to recruit new talent. A limited number of dancers are usually signed. If you don't secure representation at that time, all is not lost. An agent may remember you when a future project appears, and choose to represent you then.

Alternatively, you can secure representation by building your own connections and booking a job. Let's say you take a dance class with a particular choreographer, and at some point the choreographer asks you directly to work on an upcoming gig. Thrilling. Contact the agent of your choice and say, "I just booked a job working with so-and-so and I need representation. Will you take me on as a client?" By making the connection and getting the job, you *may* get an agent.

Agency Cred. Consider the type of work that appeals to you, and look for agencies that have a relationship with the choreographers you'd like to work with. Study an agency's existing clientele. If it already represents lots of artists who have characteristics similar to yours, that agency may not need you at this time.

Review the history, ratings, submission standards, types of artists represented, and category of jobs booked. Make sure the agency is a member of the Association of Talent Agents (ATA) and/or is franchised by one of these unions: SAG-AFTRA or Actors Equity. SAG-AFTRA provides a list of both ATA and SAG-AFTRA-franchised agents on its website: sagaftra.org.

Boutique and Local. Just because an agency has a big name doesn't mean it's the best one for you. Regardless of your age or where you live, consider the smaller, boutique agencies for finding regional work. If no local agent in your area works specifically with dancers, look for one that represents other types of artists. Such agents can help you prepare for auditions and gain work experience close to home. Think local TV and print ads—or even industrials.

Submission and Interview. Most agencies have an online submission protocol. That is, you may send video links for their review. Be sure to send a video in which you can be clearly seen, since it's too much of a challenge when you say, "I'm the third from the left, wearing the black shorts."

Upfront Money. No matter how anxious or excited you are, never pay upfront fees to an agent, manager, casting director, or modeling agency. This includes referrals for classes or for photographers. Fees are to be negotiated independently between you and the service provider.

If something sounds too good to be true, think twice. Look elsewhere. No legitimate agent or manager will ever suggest or ask for an upfront payment to secure employment.

"SO TELL ME A LITTLE ABOUT YOURSELF."

Agents need to determine if you're a fit with them. For them to discern who you are as an artist and as an individual, prepare for their requests for details about you. There are no wrong answers. Talk about your dance history, the kind of dancer you are, who you want to work with, and about your dream job. Share your intentions so that they can best advise you.

If agents can't help you transition from the artist you currently are to the artist you want to be, it doesn't make sense for them to add you to their roster and then leave your file sitting in a box.

Your Headshots. Industry practices and protocols regarding marketing materials change. Your headshot is probably your number one marketing tool, aside from your physical skill. Agents typically ask for two photos: a traditional headshot, and a full-body shot that showcases your style and physicality, and represents you as a dancer. Whether you're more a Nickelodeon-type dancer or are interested in jobs with VH1 or MTV, your photos need to represent or portray that. So dress, style, and pose yourself for the part you want.

Your Résumé. Most agencies offer samples and sites to help you with digital and print versions of your résumé. Your address, education, high school name, or Social Security number are of little concern to casting agents. Instead, they're interested in your name, height, hair color, eye color, "portrayable" ethnicity, and body type.

If you're just starting out and lack professional credits, provide some idea of your skills in performing, as well as your training. List all the performances you've been a part of, your role in them (singer, dancer, soloist, etc.), and the directors, production companies, and/or choreographers you've worked for.

Include competitions, local or high school performances, and any work you've done for TV, theater, industrials, film, or dance teams. You should also include professional trainings, education programs, licenses, certifications or degrees, etc. Provide your agent as the point of contact to protect your private information. If you don't yet have an agent, then provide your email address and your website (if you have one).

When listing your special skills (such as combat, harness work, aerials, rollerblading, hula hoop, pointe, tumbling), *do not* list any skill you don't actually have. In addition to tarnishing your name and making you appear unprofessional, this can have a negative ripple effect on scheduling, talent rebooking, wardrobe, insurance, location permits, etc. Not booking a job is one thing; but booking a job you can't actually do results in time-consuming and costly production complications.

Of Age. Many agents advise and even encourage those wanting to pursue a career as a professional dancer to move to a big city like LA or New York after they've turned 18. Before you act on this, though, consider the pros and cons carefully. (See the chapter titled "Relocation Navigation.")

YOUR BEST CYBER SELF.

Promoting yourself and the work you do requires a deft and nimble approach. While you want to do it in a manner that distinguishes you as unique among others in your field, effective self-promotion requires finding the right balance between "over-promoting" and "under-promoting." The former can come across as shameless bragging, and the latter can make you forgettable.

Careful What You Click For. Dancers do book jobs from activity online and, in fact, many casting notices request that you add your social media accounts when submitting applications. You'd be surprised how quickly and profoundly just a tiny bit of personal information can affect your career. What you post and promote and the methods in which you do so can either hinder or help your career. Post valuable content, not just the stuff that makes you look a certain way. Be genuine and support others by showing a sincere interest in what they share. (By the way, just because something can be shared doesn't mean it needs to be.)

Now You're Clicking. Increase your visibility, build an audience, and generate interest in what you do by leveraging digital tools. Consider making your tweets, blogs, clips, reels, and other online content links easily accessible. Lead viewers to a central home base, such as your YouTube page, website, or any other place where people can keep up-to-date with the latest and greatest on what's happening with you and your evolving career.

COMMUNICATION.

Your relationship with your agent, like any partnership, depends in part on you. Think of the relationship as working like puzzle pieces coming together, in that the more you connect with your agent, the more the whole picture falls into place. Then, from there the momentum builds. That's because the more your agent "gets" you, the more work your agent can get you.

Drop In. Technically, agents work for you, their client—not the other way around. It's O.K. to express a concern, even if you do feel intimidated. It's all right to say, "It's slow. What's going on? Is there anything I need to do? Is there something I should be doing more of? Or less of?"

By asking questions like these, you show that you're open to using whatever feedback you receive to take your game up a level. Maintain open communication, and keep your agent apprised of your schedule, newly acquired skills, projects, and accomplishments. The ultimate in client-agent success can be found in this Henry Ford quote: "Coming together is the beginning. Keeping together is progress. Working together is success."

Get comfortable enough to walk in and talk openly with your agent about your career. When visiting, set the tone and the agenda through your words. If you're there to say, "Thanks—and here's a box of chocolates because you went out of your way to get me that job I wanted," that's great.

However, gifts aren't necessary, and the notion of gift-giving as a way to get noticed by agents doesn't work. On the other hand, expressions of kindness, sincerity, or verbal appreciation go a long way. Also, if you're performing in a local showcase, invite your agent.

Out Of Sight, Out Of Mind. If your agent has to ask, "What have you been up to?" you're either not sufficiently visible or you're insufficiently communicating. If, when asked, you have little to report, consider doing something worth talking about. After all, creativity is the substance of show business. Invest in your career and an agent will do the same.

BEFORE YOU SIGN ANY CONTRACT.

You're the one who has to commit to the dates, timelines, locations, and other terms. So, consider what you need to do (give up, trade off, or postpone) to honor the contract. Ensure that the compensation is fair and that the contract meets non-union and/or union specifications.

Read a contract carefully and write down questions and negotiation points. Run it past a third or fourth party—someone who can help you definitively understand what you will be required to do to meet every stipulated term of the contract. (If you don't have access to a lawyer, then your parent or cousin who's been studying for the bar is a good place to start.)

It's easier to get clarification on what a document says than it is to get out of an agreement you've already signed and committed to. Keep in mind that such documents as non-disclosure and confidentiality agreements are legally binding. Also, those two are generally separate forms—that is, in addition to your contract. Never sign anything under pressure or duress. And before you sign on any dotted line, read everything—especially THE SMALL PRINT.

WHAT ABOUT MANAGERS?

Managers differ from agents in a few respects. They generally represent fewer artists than agents do. They work on a more personal level with their clients. And they take a broader view concerning their clients; that is, they oversee more aspects of a performer's career. Also, managers help clients with their overall professional identities.

In addition, a manager's contract will have different terms than those of an agent, and a manager's commission can extend beyond that of an agent's 10%.

Note that many managers are unregulated and not licensed by the state or franchised by the unions.

GETTING PAID.

The more you do to advance your business, the more your agent can do to help you find work. And when you get paid, your agent gets paid. Teamwork makes it work.

Agents look to safeguard your health as well as your paycheck. They can't do that without the facts. While working a job, keep a log of the dates, start and stop times, breaks, and hours worked. This helps to ensure fair compensation.

Talk to your agent about anything at a job that you're unclear, unsure, or uneasy about.

Reputable agents are licensed and regulated by state and local government agencies. (Note, however, that this isn't the case in all states.) They earn a 10% commission for facilitating connections for you. This fee is set by state laws pertaining to talent agencies and limited by union franchise agreements. In certain instances, commissions on non-union projects can be greater than 10%. These fees are outlined in the talent representation agreement and deducted from your pre-tax earnings. (Key term: *pre-tax*.)

Bear in mind that most likely you'll work as both an employee, wherein your taxes are deducted by the payroll company (W-2 wages), and an independent contractor, wherein taxes aren't withheld (1099 wages). Also, remember that you'll have to pay taxes on all 1099 wages at the end of the year.

Ignorance of the Law Is No Excuse. It wasn't until my first of three IRS audits that I understood the importance of paying taxes on 1099 income. Not fun, and not cool. Building a career as an entrepreneur comes with responsibility. No sitting back letting accountants or lawyers make decisions for you without knowing what's going on. Study up, grasshopper. ✦

YOU ARE THE BUSINESS OF YOU. YOU DO THE FLYING. YOUR AGENT IS YOUR CO-PILOT.
Agents work hard to build a rapport and sustain good working relationships with industry professionals. Your goal once you have representation is to enhance those relationships through your professionalism, work ethic, and sunny disposition.

13. UNIONS AND OTHER SUPPORT ORGANIZATIONS

Our labor unions are not narrow, self-seeking groups. They have raised wages, shortened hours, and provided supplemental benefits. Through collective bargaining and grievance procedures, they have brought justice and democracy to the shop floor.

~ John F. Kennedy

To work in the industry you're under no obligation to join a union, and it's possible to book non-union work. In some instances, if you're part of a union you may be prevented from accepting non-union work. But, companies hiring performers without union contracts aren't obligated to follow union guidelines that are meant to protect you.

With non-union gigs, for example, it's difficult to predict what the pay rate will be. In some cases, dancers may be compensated for rehearsals and performances. In other cases, compensation applies only to the performances—and it's likely the pay won't be a union-approved rate. Non-union projects generally have tighter budgets, lower pay, looser working conditions, and no healthcare benefits.

MEMBERSHIP.

Each union has its own requirements, restrictions, dues, fees, and structures. Which one you join will depend on the type of jobs you book. Every job is different, and every union is different as far as who and what it represents.

In some cases, you can be non-union when you audition for a union gig. If you book the job, you'll be given a certain amount of time to join the union.

Be aware that union membership increases your chances of receiving union jobs.

AEA. Most jobs on Broadway, in television, and in film are union jobs. For instance, if you book a Broadway gig, joining the Actors' Equity Association (AEA) is a must. The AEA is an affiliate of the AFL-CIO, the largest federation of unions in the country. This union represents around 50,000 stage managers and actors. It's dedicated to protecting and advancing the careers of its members. Musical theater and opera performers also are commonly members of the AEA.

AGVA. Every Rockette at Radio City in New York is a member of the American Guild of Variety Artists (AGVA), which is also an AFL-CIO-affiliated labor union. The AGVA was established to represent performers working in theme parks, circuses, cabarets, variety shows, dance revues, and special events.

AGMA. Ballet and modern company dancers, as well as concert musicians, are represented by the American Guild of Musical Artists (AGMA), a branch of the Associated Actors and Artists of America. Around 7,500 artists and production staff are represented by this national union.

SAG-AFTRA. If you book a commercial or television episode, or have completed a certain number of union jobs, you'll have to join SAG-AFTRA. Commercial dancers typically do. Other members of this union include film and television principals, background performers, journalists, and radio personalities.

SUPPORT GROUPS.

Support groups differ from unions in that they come in the form of alliances, foundations, funds, clubs, organizations, non-profits, charities, and professional associations. Each one offers different career and personal enrichment services. Broadway Cares, Dancers Over 40, The Dance Fund, Stage Directors and Choreographers Society, Motion Picture & Television Fund, Union Plus, and Global Dance Initiative are some of our support groups. Here are descriptions of a few others.

The Actors Fund of America (AFOA). This is a national nonprofit organization dedicated to the welfare of entertainers who work in the arts onstage, on camera, and behind the scenes. Among the many services the AFOA provides are emergency financial assistance, health insurance, counseling, support groups, and help with affordable housing. Their tagline is "Helping dancers across the country to thrive during all phases of their careers." Career Transition for Dancers is a program within The Actors Fund. It offers career counseling, scholarships, small business grants, national dance community outreach, and more.

Professional Dancers Society (PDS). This is a nonprofit corporation whose goal is to serve both active and inactive professional dancers. It's an affiliate of The Actors Fund of America. PDS provides dancers with a variety of social services, and financial assistance for housing, medical, and other emergency needs. Joe Tremaine has served on its board for the past 30 years. He invites friends to attend the annual Gypsy Awards Luncheon, which serves as PDS's major fundraising event for The Actor's Fund.

Dancers Alliance. This is a national collective dedicated to mentoring, and directing community outreach. The group is composed of dancers and agents who support and protect the rights of all dancers to receive fair wages and working conditions.

IN SERVICE TO YOUR FELLOW ARTISTS.

Unions and support groups are made up primarily of artists who, like you, love our industry. Educate yourself about how these groups and organizations create positive change for our communities and our industry.

Stay open to the idea of one day making your contribution through serving and supporting the welfare and interests of your fellow artists.

For Us, By Us. I didn't know much about unions or support groups when I arrived in Los Angeles. My first gig on *The Gregory Hines Show* provided me with eligibility to join what was then the Screen Actors Guild (SAG). SAG has since joined forces with the American Federation of Television and Radio Artists (AFTRA), thus creating SAG-AFTRA, of which I remain a proud dues-paying member. ✦

THE GOALS OF UNIONS AND SUPPORT GROUPS MAY OVERLAP, BUT THEY RESPECT EACH OTHER'S *LABORS.*

14. CAREERS BEHIND THE CURTAIN

You have brains in your head. You have feet in your shoes.
You can steer yourself any direction you choose.

~ Dr. Seuss

Whether you plan to teach, perform, film, blog, podcast, costume, direct, or choreograph, ultimately it's about getting or creating jobs you love. Job equals money, money equals freedom, and freedom equals more time and opportunity to grow as an artist.

Artists support one another. While one person performs, another teaches or choreographs. While one artist is onstage, another is out of the limelight designing or manufacturing costumes. While a sound technician operates the soundboard, a tap dancer's taps are heard over the music. Whether you're behind the camera, a special effects makeup artist, an agent, or a medical professional supporting other dancers, we need you.

Toward the Illogical. Everywhere I go—and I go a lot of places—I see example after example of exactly how much many of you who have come up through dance have accomplished. Most of us started out pretty much the same way: taking recreational classes at a local studio. Then we fell in love with dance as a hobby and, sooner or later, realized we couldn't imagine doing anything else with our lives.

I run into dancers who have started businesses, organizations, charities, clinics, foundations, costume companies, and a whole lot of other endeavors all designed around their particular love for the arts.

Dance trains us for life. To me, that is just phenomenal. To think that we all came up the same way and go on to use our dance training to build fulfilling lives and careers is remarkable. What could be better than honing your skills and going on to become part of the "Who's Who" of our great industry?

One such influential industry leader is Jamie King. I remember giving Jamie a convention scholarship when he was about fifteen years old. Today he's considered live music's most respected and most sought-after director and choreographer in the world. From Prince to Madonna to Cirque du Soleil and so many more, Jamie's work has earned more than $5 billion in ticket sales. Jamie is a creative director, choreographer, and producer who directs concert tours for pop stars. In July of 2011, *Variety* published a 12-page, career tribute issue naming Jamie a "Billion-Dollar Tour Director."

During one of our phone conversations, Jamie made the statement, "Move toward the illogical." I love that expression. To me, it means using your imagination and believing in all the possibilities. It's about going beyond ordinary.

None of us can see the entire big picture for our lives, but we can usually figure out enough to know whether or not we should turn right or left. With direction comes some certainty. And with certainty, we have enough ammunition to strive past any doubts (if they happen to exist). Moves towards the illogical. ✦

SHOW
BUSINESS, LIKE
LIFE ITSELF,
HAS NO
CLEAR-CUT
SET OF
DIRECTIONS.
YOU WON'T
FIND A
ONE-SIZE-FITS-
ALL STRATEGY.

DANCE LEADS TO MANY FORMS OF SELF-EXPRESSION.
CHOOSE YOUR ADVENTURE.

There are many doorways into show biz. Every performer's journey is different. No two dancers share identical charisma, boldness, or levels of commitment. Your options for executing your talents behind the curtain are limitless.

Your skills and the way you express yourself will ultimately determine what works for you. Go on an adventure balancing multiple ideas and goals. You'll likely find expertise in more than one area of your life.

CHARTING YOUR COURSE.

Expand your scope. Explore the periphery and look to connect the dots—or cross-pollinate ideas—to see how your other interests might relate to dance. Discover other passions you may not know you have, and keep looking to match your talents to your interests.

In the first chart below, identify the skills and expertise you've acquired through your dance training. Then look at all the career options in the categorized lists that follow. In which areas would your skills and expertise be relevant?

Retire? Never! When asked about retirement, I let people know right away that the answer is *never*. Why would I stop doing what I love? There's no stopping.

Retread or change directions? Yes. I reinvent myself, change channels, and transition through career phases. That's what I do. Dance has no mandatory retirement age. Thank goodness for that. ✦

15. DANCE STUDIO OWNERSHIP

*In a completely rational society, the best of us would be teachers
and the rest of us would have to settle for something else.*

~ Lee Iacocca

Studio ownership is the cornerstone of our industry, and dance teachers are its foundation. Someday you may consider entering one of the noblest of professions by teaching at and owning your very own dance studio. To that end, we approached friends who have owned a studio for at least ten years and asked for their opinions on what you should know. Their responses follow.

1. **Always remember why you chose this profession.** Remember where you came from, and what or who inspired your passion. Pass on to your students what was given to you. Dance is an art—so create artists, not competition professionals. (Those storage closets full of trophies, medals, and plaques? All they really do is take up valuable space.)

2. **Project yourself into the future.** Think about what you would want your former students and their parents to say about you. Would you want them to say, "Not only did I get a great dance education, but also I *mattered*. My experience there gave me self-esteem and other awesome benefits"? Or do you want them to say, "We won a lot of trophies"? Run your business with the answers of those (future former) students and their parents in mind.

3. **Have a clear mission statement and stick to it.** Review it occasionally and make adjustments. When students (or their parents) get confused or question your direction, send your mission statement to them in an email. Make sure it reflects a philosophy you truly believe in, then don't stray from that philosophy to please someone. Your individuality is what clients—actual and potential—will be drawn to, and if you change to accommodate people, you'll lose what makes your business unique among all other studios.

4. **Stay true to your principles.** When you create the guidelines for your studio, read them as though you were a parent. If it were your child, would you want her to dance there? Are your guidelines inviting, or are they bossy and uncaring? If you're satisfied with what you've written, stick to it and stay true to your principles. Parents want the best for their children, and acknowledging their concerns defuses many situations quickly. Yet don't let parents dictate how you run your studio, or allow them to participate in studio management. This is *your* dream. Stick to how you want to do it, and make it what you want it to be.

5. **Maintain your sanity.** Understand your clients, and do what you can to please them without sacrificing your values and who you are as a person. (Be O.K. with saying *no*. Keep true to yourself—it's *your* studio.) Cut out any negativity ASAP, and get beyond fears of criticism or of loss. As a business owner, you're a leader, and because of this people will talk about you. If the talk is negative, you may possibly lose students and families. Through it all, be sure to monitor your stress levels. By maintaining your sanity you'll maintain your business.

6. **Remember: *profit* isn't a dirty word.** Owning a dance studio doesn't have to be a hobby. You can create artists, teach students to love dance, and still put food on the table. It's a business. You're the CEO and you need to treat your business as such. So study up on relevant topics such as business methods, customer service, marketing, and finances. Ensure that your website is up-to-date and that all your social media accounts are active and engaging. Also make sure that every element on your website represents your studio in a flattering way. You have to be a business owner and care about the gritty numbers. *Free* is not an option. Give yourself value. Making exceptions as to who pays fees is not good for you or your clients. If possible, have a good office manager who can deal with parents. Separate emotions from business decisions; and if you can't, hire someone to manage the business aspect of things. Let someone else handle collecting funds if your heart gets in the way.

7. **Change with the times.** What worked in the past isn't guaranteed to work in the future. Yes, you're the studio owner. But, remember that you'll learn so much from your students (and their parents) if you keep your eyes and heart open. Also, listen to your teachers: They're the ones who teach the students, and they see more than you do.

8. **Create a loving environment.** Keep in mind that you're not only offering a dance education, you're also being a mentor and helping students develop life skills. It's about creating a place that others can call home. Be a dance family… and don't forget about your own family at home. They need you too.

9. **Delegate.** You'll be a plumber, janitor, sound tech, psychologist, and parent… all before you teach the first class. Delegate, and let go of perfectionist tendencies. Life never goes exactly as planned, but somehow it's still O.K. It helps to keep in mind that we studio owners have the best job: We help mold the next generation by passing on the love of dance.

10. **Ooze love and respect.** Your students are not your property, so no one can "steal" them from you. Rather, they're your clients. If you treat them with respect and dedication, they'll continue to believe in, and invest in, your services with confidence.

11. **Pay attention to the child who retreats to the back corner.** Bring that student forward one day to demonstrate—it will change her or his dance life. Some of our "worst" students have gone on to make careers in dance. Never give up on any student. We all flourish in our own time.

12. **Share your success.** Not only is it O.K., it's *important* for you to be friends with other studio owners. They're the ones who understand what you're going through. Share your success and create good working relationships with them. Be vocal about your respect for how other studio owners do what they do, and never talk negatively about them—or about other teachers, for that matter—in front of your dancers or their parents. (Just because other people don't do everything the same way you do doesn't mean their ways don't have value.)

CLEAR BRANDING. CLEAR STANDING.

If you do open your own dance studio, find your niche, keep your product fresh, and maintain your standards so that you'll make your school a destination for the kind of people you want to do business with.

Snap. My dearest dance teachers, I have a note of advisement regarding one peculiar side effect of years of teaching, counting, and snapping your fingers. I recently applied to TSA for their fingerprinting program. I drove all the way to LAX from Hollywood. I picked the perfect time of day because the I-405 was smooth sailing. Parking was a breeze, and I walked right in. There wasn't even a line.

Things were going my way until the TSA workers had to spend 45 minutes trying to capture my prints. More and more employees gathered around us, all baffled. I could tell this was new for them. Finally, one of them said, "Mr. Tremaine, we can't find your fingerprints." I wiggled my hands in the air and said, "What do you mean you can't find 'em? They're right here on the tips of my fingers." They suggested that I go to their downtown office to try again.

Now, if you know me, you know I don't do nobody's downtown nothing. I might shop Los Angeles Avenue for a glitzy gala jacket, but that's about it. So anyway... leave it to me to be the person with no prints. Right?

It was time for me to get the heck outta there. As I headed to the door, I had one of those *aha!* moments. I knew why they couldn't find my prints. Right when I reached the door, I pivoted around and gave the whole group of TSA workers a chassé with a little pas de bourrée into a pose. I hit my mark and said, confident as could be, "I know what happened to my fingerprints. I've been dancing and snapping my fingers my whole life. I'm a jazz dancer, and I very obviously snapped the prints right off my fingers."

They looked at me like I was crazy, which didn't faze me one bit. I walked back to my car with pride and joy. I said to myself, "So that's the side effect of teaching all these years, eh? Well, if that's the price this shy boy from the cotton fields of Louisiana has to pay for doing what he loves, then I'll gladly pay it." ✦

"... 5, 6, 7, 8!"
WHO DO WE
APPRECIATE?
A ROUND OF
APPLAUSE
FOR DANCE
EDUCATORS!

SECTION 4

PERSONAL POWER

16. HIGHER EDUCATION

The beautiful thing about learning is that no one can take it away from you.

~ B.B. King

We, the authors of this book, attended college, remain forever grateful for the experience, and advocate higher education for about 98% of the kids we see and train. The other 2% are superstars with talents so extraordinary and amazingly undeniable that going directly into the business is an obvious first choice. These artists make a name for themselves and quickly receive offers to be hired, promoted, represented, and, in some cases, funded.

"Only the educated are free." These are the words of Epictetus, an ancient Greek who was a big deal in the Stoic school of philosophy. I love this quote because I believe that education gives you options.

In one of the most-watched TED Talks, creativity and education expert Sir Ken Robinson asserted that students' creativity is stifled by sitting in classrooms for seven hours a day learning math, science, and English. I agree with him 100%—not that he needs my approval. He wondered what would happen if students spent equal amounts of time dancing, drawing, and singing as they do studying academics. I can answer that question: The world would be a much more beautiful place.

I've always loved learning, yet I went to college only because my father insisted on it. The day after my college graduation—the very next day—I handed my sheepskin diploma to my father (back then they were actually made of sheepskin), and I booked a ride as fast as I could out of the cotton fields of Louisiana to New Orleans so I could continue dancing. I have a degree in sociology. A lot of good that's doing me.

I realize now that a degree in business with a minor in marketing would have been a better choice. But, oh well… nothing I can do about that now. I have my BA, and in retrospect I'm glad my father made me go.

If you're undecided about college and can afford the tuition, I say go. Education and academic development will enhance your life and give you time to mature and learn who you are! ◆

"Don't leave me here!" I ran after my mom's car as she drove away from my college campus. She pulled over and stopped long enough for me to repeat what I'd been saying for days: "Please don't leave me here. I don't want to go to this school or any other school!" Her reply that day was one of the pivotal moments of my life. She said, "Look. All I ask is that you stay one week. After that, you decide. But stay this week and feel the experience for and within yourself. If it's not for you, then you can leave. I want you to stay because I don't want you to say you didn't have the *opportunity* to go to college."

College was my wake-up call in two serious ways. One, it made me quickly comprehend why family members and teachers had referred to me for years as a first-class, cloud-niner, out-to-lunch daydreamer. Two, it exposed me to just how unexposed

I was. I spent a good amount of time in a state of shock as to how academically and socially deficient I was. I wanted to run away from the challenges I knew college presented. But an education helped me see the world through fresh eyes, in a way a non-academic setting would never have revealed to me. Running is the answer if you're on the track team, not so much in life. Thank goodness Mother stopped the car that day... otherwise, I might still be running. ✦

GAIN HIGHER EDUCATION WITHOUT SETTING FOOT ON A COLLEGE CAMPUS.

COLLEGE BOUND.

If college is something you've always wanted to pursue, and you're adequately motivated and disciplined to make the most of the experience, research and visit (physically or virtually) as many schools as possible. Exhaust every effort to gauge which places you would do well at. Knowledge is power and the more you know about the subject before making a decision, the more likely it is that your decision will be a good one. Gather information on obvious details such as location, distance from your home, expenses (including living costs), admission requirements, and potential debt. If you're trying to select the right dance degree program and school, check out *Dance Magazine*'s "College Guide."

FORGOING TRADITIONAL EDUCATION.

For some people, their life experiences and their own ideas have a greater pull, and college doesn't play a part in their stories. But, because a person doesn't attend college doesn't mean he or she stops learning. Respected people from Abraham Lincoln to Will Smith, from Walt Disney and Ellen DeGeneres to Mark Zuckerberg didn't attend college. They did, however, receive a higher education—it simply wasn't in the traditional sense.

MAKING THE GRADE.

If you don't attend a traditional college, you can self-direct your education. Community colleges, trade schools, or apprenticeship programs are affordable and flexible options for learning. Other tools and platforms include websites like CreativeLive, Skillshare, and Khan Academy. Massive open online courses (MOOCs), online universities, and other self-directed options let you customize and design your own à la carte curriculum.

Self-directed education provides scheduling flexibility and manageable tuition costs. You have the power to create unique learning experiences to meet your interests.

A YEAR OF SELF-DISCOVERY.

It's easier to try new things while you're young and more fearless about life—at a time when you probably have fewer financial or family obligations. A gap year, typically taken between high school and college, is an opportunity to venture out and discover more about yourself.

Before considering the possibility of a gap year, though, reflect on your goals, your level of maturity, and what you're prepared and committed to take on. The years pass quickly.

Here's a mere sampling of what you could do:

Life's a trip. Mark Twain noted that, "Travel is fatal to prejudice, bigotry, and narrow-mindedness." Nothing can replace the unique experiences of voyaging to distant lands, learning new languages, eating different foods, and dancing with new mates.

Doing good is its own reward. Serve others through community or volunteer efforts. The opportunities are endless, and you can pretty much find a volunteer project that suits you in any city you like. Maybe advocate for a cause in areas such as global poverty, homelessness, domestic abuse, elder care, or animal rights. Perhaps join a union or other organization that supports safe working environments, fair wages, and insurance for dancers. Teaching dance or movement classes in an assisted-living facility is another option. Perhaps a wildlife conservation job or working on an expedition for renewable energy is more your thing. The very act of giving benefits you and marks the beginning of the receiving.

Cruise control. Travel the world, perform, meet new people, and make money by dancing on a cruise ship. Working at a theme park provides similar benefits and results (except for traveling the world, of course).

Get a job. Heck. Work a couple of part-time gigs. You may not love them all, but you may discover and develop talents you didn't know you had. You may not immediately find ways to completely nourish yourself by doing what you love to do, but try to find work in areas of interest to you.

It's an enormous responsibility to begin new a phase of life, and planning your future can feel overwhelming. But begin you must. If you find yourself trapped between your dreams and what other people want for you, follow your own happy path without caving in to outside pressure. Making everyone else happy and neglecting your own ideals does not make for a pleasant life.

17. HEALTH IS WEALTH

A fit, healthy body—that is the best fashion statement.

~ Jess C. Scott

Our life spans are getting longer and so are our dance careers. As human performance evolves, our bodies can perform physical feats beyond previous limits. We jeté higher, run faster, balance longer, and throw farther. We train more effectively than people did a century ago. We have more scientifically designed, better enhanced shoes, clothing, flooring, and other equipment. We know more about exercise philosophies and advances in health, nutrition, medicine, and technology, and our knowledge allows us to perform beyond the physical limits of our predecessors. It's not uncommon to see dancers performing and teaching well into their seventies, eighties, and beyond.

A WEALTH OF FITNESS METHODS.

Fitness is crucial to your overall well-being, and different routines offer distinctive benefits throughout your life and career. The fitter you are, the more likely you'll continue to perform, both onstage and offstage, at optimal levels.

There's a common misconception that dancers are always in shape and therefore don't need to bother with other forms of physical fitness. We may be ahead of the curve due to our regular physical training, but we still need to incorporate other forms of exercise into our regimens.

If your principal form of physical activity is dance, the International Association for Dance Medicine and Science has this to say: A well-rounded dance training program must be comprised of all components of fitness.

Aerobic Fitness: moderate, longer levels of activity

Anaerobic Fitness: high-intensity, short bursts of activity

Muscle Endurance: strength and power (speed)

Flexibility: the range of motion at a joint in association with the pliability of a muscle

Neuromuscular Coordination: balance, agility, coordination, and skill

Body Composition: the makeup of body weight by percentage of muscle and fat

Rest: recovery and regeneration

IT'S EASIER TO STAY IN SHAPE THAN IT IS TO GET (BACK) IN SHAPE.

Pay attention to the needs of your body, and explore the variety of components and the range of tools that each type of fitness method has to offer.

For example, aerobics improves stamina and endurance, while plyometric and interval training helps you gain power, energy, and jumping capacity. If strengthening your core is important, then Pilates might be ideal. If you're already hyper-mobile, then yoga may not be the best choice for you.

Pilates and core-strengthening classes are *fitness-for-dancers* regimens that complement dancing. Zumba and cardio-barre are two types of *dance fitness* classes for people who want to improve their fitness by incorporating some dance exercise into their routines.

Cross-training options like cycling, swimming, elliptical, and steps provide different benefits to different people. Zero in on the components that will be most advantageous to your wellness as you unite the strength-training techniques found in the world of fitness with your dance training and technique.

StairMaster. If you want to be taken seriously in the dance world, it helps to look and feel your best. That's going to be different for each of us, and you have to work with what you've got. Find a regimen that works best for you, and take good care of your body. Don't ever take it for granted.

I meet with a personal trainer a couple of times each week, and part of my regimen is to climb a lot of stairs. As a kid, I accidentally locked myself in a closet. Hours went by before I was rescued and, as a result, I'm claustrophobic. I don't do MRIs and I don't take elevators. There have been occasions when I've climbed 20-plus flights of stairs just to get to a doctor appointment. Of course, by the time I got there it was obvious I could skip the stress test. ◆

IF YOU WANT TO BE TAKEN SERIOUSLY IN THE DANCE WORLD, IT HELPS TO LOOK AND FEEL YOUR BEST.

Hurdles Are Complications Dressed In Gym Clothes. When I'm traveling from city to city with Tremaine Dance Conventions, the first thing I do after walking into my hotel room is put on my sneakers and march right back out of the room heading for the gym.

Sometimes I'm too tired or not in the mood to work out. But, I walk down the hall and into the elevator, and press the button for the gym floor. And then it happens... the moment when I saunter past the weights and the ellipticals and turn right around to make my exit. When I turn around and don't work out, I'm not doing myself a disservice. I'm actually really tired.

Such is life. You can't win 'em all and nothing is guaranteed.

Committing to doing something doesn't mean you'll hit your mark with every attempt. Resist the notion that because you've done everything right, things won't go wrong. Make peace with imperfection, stay calm, and prepare to revisit the trenches in a few hours or days. You're stronger than you think. ◆

Original Parts. While on convention one weekend, I was minding my own business when out of the blue a woman approached me and asked, "Joe, do you still have all your original working parts?" Without missing a step or slowing my stride, I replied, "Yes! Last time I checked, everything was mine and working just fine. Thank you very much." Some nerve she had. ◆

Jean Therapy. I gained 25 pounds during my first two years of college. I was consumed by thoughts about my weight and about how tight my jeans felt and looked. Outgrowing your clothes is uncomfortable. But you know what's even more uncomfortable? Wearing them anyway.

My strategy for maintaining my weight back then and still today is simple. I force, yes, force myself to wear jeans even when they are too tight. I'm miserable throughout the day, and by nightfall my mood worsens. Can we talk about the horrible indentations left on my body from the tight jeans? Torture! Stretchy clothing denies me the opportunity to know what's expanding where.

My simple approach is my personal alarm to push back from the table—while I'm still able. Because it's all fun and games until your jeans won't go up past your knees. ✦

Growing Old Ain't for Sissies. If you want a long and productive life—and, like me, you have no intention of retiring—keep dancing.

Your body will change as you age, and it will benefit from different fitness regimens at different times throughout your life. You'd be wise to start thinking *now* about how you're going to balance dance, diet, and whatever else you do to maintain good health. You want to look and feel your best regardless of what you do for a living. ✦

Risk Probability. Impact Assessment. If you find yourself in a Bikram yoga class, your instructor may say something like, "You can mess with the gods, but you can't mess with the knees. The gods are more forgiving."

I'm impulsive. But when it comes to safeguarding my physical well-being, I don't play. I had two knee surgeries over a five-year period while in my thirties. The first one was the result of being hit by a car while riding my bike. The second was to repair damage from tears, stretches, and boo-boos from a previous dance injury I had never let heal properly.

To avoid problems, I've learned to just say no. During one of my crazy, all-out-summer-fun vacations in Puerto Vallarta, a local gentleman asked me to ride on the back of his motorbike. "No," I told him. He assured me it would only be a short ride to the corner and back. Again, I said, "No." The more I refused, the more he insisted. Several more rounds of adult peer pressure ensued.

Finally, as if to suggest he had authority over me, Mr. Motorbike said, "O.K. Well, at least give me one good reason why." Mr. Motorbike was a complete stranger, and it was none of his business. Besides, offering explanations can cause some people to assume you're asking for their permission or approval.

Finally, Mr. Motorbike turned his attention away from me and found a willing rider. Unfortunately for her, five minutes later she was bruised and limping from the fall they'd sustained.

I never told Mr. Motorbike why I wouldn't accept his offer, but I'll tell you: At the time, I had no medical insurance.

DANCE
SMARTER,
DANCE
LONGER.
DANCE
STRONGER,
LIVE
LONGER.
LIVE
LONGER,
DANCE
FOREVER...
AND ALL IS
RIGHT WITH
THE WORLD.

As dancers, we have the responsibility to conduct some sort of risk assessment to calculate the upside and downside of a decision. If the upside is zero, what's the point? If there's no downside, take the ride. If both exist, define the risk along with the likely, serious, and not so serious outcomes.

We're free to choose. We're not free of the consequences. ✦

. . . .

PREVENT AND PROTECT.

You appreciate love after heartache, and dance after sitting on the sidelines due to an injury. Nothing's more shattering to a dancer than an afflicted (and possibly aggrieved) body. Injury prevention is what's up.

R.I.C.E. Therapy. For acute injuries, remember "R.I.C.E. is nice." *R.I.C.E.* is an acronym for "**R**est, **I**ce, **C**ompression, and **E**levation."

Rest facilitates the healing process. Yet, too much of it can decrease mobility, cause the buildup of scar tissue, and even alter technique. Worse still, it can delay your return to the dance floor.

Ice, not heat, works in the case of trauma. Ice should be applied until the affected area is numb, which usually takes about 12–15 minutes. Ice is a great anti-inflammatory because it decreases swelling and helps localize pain in about three minutes.

Compression helps to limit and prevent further stress, and clear the area of injured cells.

Elevation reduces swelling by removing unwanted fluid and improving blood flow towards the heart.

Strength. Supporting the abdominals can help with back pain. Bolstering the glutes may alleviate knee pain. And strengthening the trapezius and rotator cuff to correct posture can relieve neck pain.

Along with good nutrition, strengthening is important in the prevention, as well as the rehabilitation, of injuries. That is, strengthening will make you less prone to injuries and, if you *are* injured, will reduce your recovery time.

FOR REAL, THOUGH.

To entertain notions from friends who say, "Well, it sounds like X, but it could be Y. Uh, I don't know. Maybe it's Z" isn't the ideal strategy. When you have an injury, consult your physician or other qualified health care provider. Therapeutic and rehabilitative approaches may include the use of props such as foam rollers, Thera-Bands, and therapy balls. These can all be great tools for the body when they're used correctly. Seek the advice of experts who specialize in fields such as chiropractic care, physical therapy, acupuncture, Reiki, cupping, and/or Yamuna Body Rolling. Consider the benefits you may derive from both Eastern and Western healing techniques. And, don't forget good old-fashioned Epsom salts with a dash of your favorite essential oils.

NUTRITION MISSION.

Eating healthy and committing to a well-maintained diet can be two of the smartest decisions you'll ever make. Nutrient-packed foods promote better health, a better mood, and enhanced energy. They also help you combat illness, reduce stress, and regulate weight. Combined with regular physical activity, a proper diet can help you feel good in the short term and, in the long term, add years to your life.

Slow Progress Is Better Than No Progress. Sticking to a healthful eating regimen may not always be easy and, like many parts in life, positive outcomes can take time. Bad habits may be difficult to break, yet tiny tweaks in the right direction can help improve your life and result in big payoffs. Fuel your body with love and healthful foods. Good health is your ultimate wealth. Eat right. Feel right.

BODY TALK.

Some days your body needs ice or a massage. Other days it may need the attention of a specialist, time off, or some other item from a very long list. Your body is smart, and it knows what's going on. For additional information on this subject, confer with an expert—one of whom is your very own body.

EATING HEALTHY AND COMMITTING TO A WELL-MAINTAINED DIET CAN BE TWO OF THE SMARTEST DECISIONS YOU'LL EVER MAKE.

Dear Dancer,

Dancing is demanding. It puts an insane amount of stress on me, your prized possession. While I am resilient, I'm also fragile, and there's only so much I can do. Aches and pains are my way of asking you nicely to please slow down, modify, or stop what you're doing.

I appreciate how you push us to explore the limits of what we can do, and I understand that you're loath to admit pain or injury. But when you make me work through pain, or take needless risks, or neglect my fatigue, it does ghastly things to me. Then you get sad and we're both down and out.

In most cases, I simply need rest. Some repetitive stress injuries are meant to heal through rest. But when you carry on, refusing to take breaks or constantly re-injuring me, it delays my recovery. Overuse slows me down and can lead to permanent damage. Overuse stalls our recovery and makes us run the risk of developing a secondary injury caused by compensating for the initial one.

And if that's not bad enough, then you go overruling my requests with coffee, energy drinks, and all your other tomfoolery. Let's not confuse pleasure with happiness. Pleasure and feeling good may come from some of your crazy quick fixes, but we both know that real happiness comes from self-actualization and meaning. Pleasures are important, but let's not get carried away. Pleasure alone won't cut it, and I don't appreciate it when you are downright reckless and imprudent. I'm always the one who's hurt and has to pay for it. Why? Why would you do this when I'm the only place you have to live?

Some of my best friends are the bodies of dancers who ignored their injuries (think: dancing through pain) or took unnecessary risks (like doing gymnastics in icy-cold rooms on concrete floors). Those bodies tell a story I don't want us to tell. To do my part, I need your cooperation. Remember teamwork? Let's stay fit. If you listen to me, kid, there's no telling how far and how long we'll go.

One final request, please. Whatever you do, don't ever, ever, ever criticize my parts. Self-deprecation, whether as a casual joke or otherwise, is not funny. The joke's really on us because where do you think all that disdainful and adverse energy goes? Hello! We live together, and I feel every iota of what you think and I believe it 100%. Your most minuscule negative thought ripples through me and gets on my last nerve—I'm telling you, it zaps the good right out of me and renders me sad.

This is the kind of avoidable nonsense that slows our progress and sets us back. I don't want any part of it. I need tender loving care. Feed me all kinds of good stuff, including love, hope, and faith. Oh, and watch your tone with me... I'm sensitive.

Sincerely,

Your beautiful, one-of-a-kind body

18. IT'S ABOUT TIME

Until we can manage time, we can manage nothing else.

~ *Peter F. Drucker*

Time makes us all equal—because we each have 24 hours in a day. Some of those hours you're awake, and you have to do what has to be done. During the remaining hours, whether you call them free time, downtime, break time, or spare time, it's all the same... precious.

Time is your ultimate, irreplaceable, and most valuable resource. Regardless of whether you have an exact or direct flight plan, going through life on autopilot is not as enjoyable as spreading your wings. Having a destination helps you choose a route. But if you don't yet have a destination, *you* are still the pilot—and time flies.

Time Change. What do you mean you have a "backup plan"? I don't care for that phrase. I never have. To me, a better way to talk about what else you can do and the skills you have to do it with is to say, "I've got skills I can rely on."

My aunt taught me how to type—and that, along with my knack for dictation and shorthand, set me apart. I could always support my dancing by *relying* on my office skills. That's what it's about. What skills can you *rely* on? Nobody's got *time* to fall back. Spring forward, for goodness sake. ✦

More Productive, Less Busy. Productivity relies on discipline and focus. Being busy? Not so much.

It's easy to be busy. I can stay busy for days, firing all my cylinders yet achieving little. I sometimes cross several items off my to-do list yet get very little accomplished. (Some items I put on my list just for the pleasure of crossing them off.)

For some of us, it's natural to want to do the fun tasks, the simpler tasks first. That's me all day. But when I have a gut-motivating goal, or if I've been told that I'm unable to accomplish something, I go all in with focus. That's when I enter the realm of productivity.

Here's an example of what I mean. I wrote my first book, *Rich by Choice, Poor by Habit,* because I was tired of, and embarrassed by, the way Joe Tremaine introduced me at the start of every competition event. My bio wasn't as exciting as those of my colleagues, many of whom had been on Broadway and traveled the world dancing. I knew I wasn't ever going to perform on Broadway, backup dance for some pop star, or tour with a dance company. I was an artist looking for ways to self-express, and writing a book allowed me to do that while differentiating myself at the same time.

Adding the title of author to my curriculum vitae took four years. Now, had I known just how ridiculously arduous it is to write a book, I probably wouldn't have started it. And once I launched the project, the process was so grueling that quitting was an

PRODUCTIVITY RELIES ON DISCIPLINE AND FOCUS. BEING BUSY? NOT SO MUCH.

everyday temptation. I managed to finish the book for one reason only: I'd told a few people what I was doing, and each of them was a bona fide busybody. You know the type. The ones who spread the word and then circle back with questions like, "So, um, yeah. What's up with that book? You still working on it?" I made them, without their knowledge, my accountability partners, and this made quitting a nonviable option.

I worked to avoid shame and embarrassment. And in the end, as overwhelmingly challenging as the project was, writing that book helped me realize that I *can* focus on one thing for more than five minutes.

Time is going to pass anyway, so why not emerge knowing you did something worthwhile with the time you were given? Working as a convention teacher requires a great deal of travel. I wrote most of this book sitting in the coach cabin of an airplane during my teaching weekends. I passed up the free upgrades to manage both weight and time—because, in the first-class cabin, I eat, snooze, and snack, while in the back of the plane, I write books on my Mac. ◆

OF ALL THAT NEEDS MANAGING IN YOUR LIFE, TIME TOPS THE LIST.

ON TASK.

Every beep, buzz, knock, or tweet is a distraction if you're trying to focus. An hour here, a distraction there… it adds up quickly. Block time out for important tasks so you can work without interruptions. Say *no* when necessary to minimize disruptions. (You'll be pleasantly surprised by how others value your time when you value it yourself.)

Furthermore, work during the part of the day when you work best. Whether you're a morning person, a night owl, or concentrate best after a dance class, figure out how to work optimally. If you occasionally fall or stall, don't allow your lack of productivity early in the day, week, or year to justify the same behavior for the rest of the day, week, or year.

THAT'S A STRETCH.

Although it may feel efficient, multitasking is anything but. You're fooling yourself if you believe you can do two things at once. Realistically, the best you can do is perform a mediocre job on both of them.

Set priorities and apply yourself to one job at a time. Divvying up your attention between tasks divides your focus, which diminishes the quality of what you're doing. Identify your most important task and focus on it until it's complete—or at least at a logical stopping point. Then decide what's next, and put all of your attention on that until it's accomplished.

Even when you're moving from one high-energy task to another, take a break between them. It's counterproductive to refuse to give your brain a rest. It takes less time to do something when you do it right the first time. Half-stepping with shortcuts, or delivering shoddy work, wastes time in the long run. Besides, the only shortcut worth taking is the one to happiness—which, as you may already know, is dancing.

YOU'RE FOOLING YOURSELF IF YOU BELIEVE YOU CAN DO TWO THINGS AT ONCE. REALISTICALLY, THE BEST YOU CAN DO IS PERFORM A MEDIOCRE JOB ON BOTH OF THEM.

IGNORE THE LITTLE DISTRACTIONS. FOCUS ON YOUR BIG DREAMS.

APPS THAT ARE APT TO BE USEFUL.

Technology and cloud-centric options provide tools and techniques for the purpose of managing your minutes. To avoid procrastination, increase productivity, and/or manage your time more wisely, consider using one of these apps.

Evernote. Keeps notes, thoughts, ideas, articles, links to video clips, and web pages in one place so you can go to them whenever you want. It's helpful for people who need to write down their ideas so they won't forget them—and it's Laurie Johnson's go-to app for staying organized.

Any.do. Switches from your phone to your laptop and helps you keep your schedule on track. It uses reminders and to-do lists. A great feature is that you can share and assign tasks to other people. (You can do anything, but you can't do everything.)

30/30. Allows you to see how long it really takes to do something—it uses timers to aid you when you want to complete certain tasks in a timely matter.

Rescue Time. Helps you figure out your daily computer and online habits so you can be aware of which tasks you spend the most time on. It will alert you to let you know how much time you spend on a particular activity. Then, for example, you can block distracting websites—the ones that really suck up your hours—by choosing a certain number of minutes to devote to each of them.

YOU DON'T FIND TIME; YOU *MAKE* TIME.

Smart Dancer: I want to get a degree in physical therapy, but I don't want to go to school for another three years.

Wise Dancer: What are you waiting for? What's the holdup?

Smart Dancer: I don't know. I think about going back to school, but by the time I graduate in three years, I'll be 30 years old.

Wise Dancer: Oh. Well, how old will you be in three years if you *don't* go back to school?

Too Bad. Too Sad. First and foremost, don't tell me your problems. If you want to go back to school, go back to school. Excuses are self-defeating. I for one don't have time to hear how you don't have time. You're wasting time even talking about it. Dillydallying as you wait for the stars to align or the ducks to form a row from stage right to stage left—those things are not going to happen.

It's about habits. Your habits move you either closer to or farther from what you want. And whatever you want, go all in and stay motivated. Let nothing stand in your way.

When you do the work, you get it all back. Hard work pays off in self-pride and happiness. That's what it's all about... on every level.

One fact to always keep in mind: Life takes time, and you'll have some rough spots, but you'll make it through. We all do. At least, most of us do. ✦

WE ARE NOT IN REHEARSAL.

I'm in Rehearsal. I daydream, gaze at shiny objects, zone out quickly, and take breaks often. Because of this, I frequently ask myself questions like *Am I making good use of my time right now? Is what I'm doing moving me closer toward a goal? When I go to bed tonight, will I be O.K. with all the piddling I'm doing right now?* Often the answer to these questions is *no*—and that's all right by me. I have no plans for 24/7 productivity. Daydreams are my rehearsal space for choreographing life.

Regarding time: I need to be aware of where it's going. While every moment, activity, or action may not create value, it helps me to know where the time goes.

I once tracked exactly how I spent each 30-minute increment for 30 days. It was sad yet eye-opening to discover how many unproductive hours I'd been squandering on the consumption of low-value content. In fact, I'd reached the point where I knew more about what a celebrity ate for lunch than I knew about the ingredients in my own food.

Then, I had a revelation: High-quality, intelligent information is just as accessible as low-value, frivolous information. I upped my Google searches and started giving my attention to what I was doing instead of keeping up with the lives of the rich and famous. I began to connect to goals, rather than to the latest fads, trends, and gossip. I stopped feeding my mind a constant barrage of junk and sensationalism.

Don't get me wrong. I don't try to master every minute, because I'm all about streaming a series. I take breaks to refresh, recharge, reflect, rejuvenate, reevaluate, recalibrate, and rhinestone. (Yes, *rhinestone* as a verb.) I break, on average, five minutes out of every 20... while I'm sure Joe breaks 20 minutes out of every five hours. ✦

STARVE THE DISTRACTIONS. FEED YOUR FOCUS.

Best in (Aquatic) Show. During my downtime I play with my dogs, who are my greatest joy in life next to dancing. I like to watch them swim in my pool. Axl, a wire hair fox terrier, transitioned in September of 2016. Gumbo is my fourth dog of this breed. Along with his younger brother Boudin, Gumbo swims and keeps me entertained. Slick Head was my first curly-coated retriever, Zeke was my second, and Boogie Woogie my third. I post videos of their backyard shenanigans at facebook.com/joe.tremaine.3. ✦

I POST VIDEOS OF THEIR BACKYARD SHENANIGANS AT FACEBOOK.COM/ JOE.TREMAINE.3.

The Scroll Marked II. I've tried reading books with pages full of words, but I lose my place, forget what I've read, and my lips get tired.

The Greatest Salesman in the World is my kind of book: small, to the point, and lightweight. The author, Og Mandino, instructs readers to read Scroll I three times a day for 30 consecutive days. After completing 30 days of reading Scroll I, then you continue to Scroll II, and so forth through Scroll X.

This book marked the beginning of my powerful transformation from cynic to optimist. I've read this book twice due to the depth of the concepts, principles, and philosophies presented. The greatest benefit of this book was that I began to understand the concept of daily discipline. It's easy to verbally commit to doing something. But it's difficult to put forth the effort necessary to develop a disciplined approach to modifying a habit. Late at night, when I was tired and didn't feel like reading for two lousy minutes, I would say to myself, "Only a loser won't invest a few minutes in her own personal development. I'm not a loser. So where did I put that book?"

The concepts are powerful, and the discipline required to read the book as prescribed was challenging. This book is not for everyone. If you don't believe that your attitude, beliefs, and habits shape your life, you may read it and have a good laugh. I did initially.

Scroll II reads, "I will greet this day with love in my heart." Get your own copy. Find out for yourself how this old-school, cool book with the word *Salesman* in the title teaches entrepreneurship and persistence. ✦

> IT'S EASY TO VERBALLY COMMIT TO DOING SOMETHING. BUT IT'S DIFFICULT TO PUT FORTH THE EFFORT NECESSARY TO DEVELOP A DISCIPLINED APPROACH TO MODIFYING A HABIT.

No Time to Dine. As a kid, my mother struggled to get me to eat. I would ask, "Isn't there a pill I can take instead?" I said this because I didn't want to stop dancing.

Today, I eat the same few items day after day, with little regard for what's on the menu. Food just isn't that important to me. As a result, I'm extremely time-efficient when it comes to dietary matters.

Give me a plain croissant, a chicken breast, and broccoli, asparagus, or potatoes. No red meat, please. Oh, and I don't want the different foods touching while on my plate. (Don't judge me.) I love ice cream—that's my weakness. I like a few tiny pieces of ice in my red wine, and I'll drink an occasional Coke. That's it. Clean and simple. And if you happen to hand me a bottle of water, make sure it's unopened. I don't know where your hands have been. ✦

19. LET'S TALK MONEY

Money without brains is always dangerous.

~ Napoleon Hill

The issue of money is far too complex for a complete review here. Yet as artists and, to varying degrees, entrepreneurs, we have a unique fiscal responsibility to manage our individual talents as a business.

Effectively budgeting, tracking, investing, and saving are essential skills for an artist. Fortunately, neither financial literacy nor fundamental money management has to be complicated or intimidating. What follows are some tips and techniques that can help you in maneuvering through your financial world.

LITTLE BECOMES MUCH.

Little acorns grow into mighty oaks, and no amount is too small to save or invest. Savings and investment vehicles exist for all income levels, and the younger you are, the more time your money will have to grow.

Nice Save. Forget the "I'll save more when I make more" approach. Always and without exception, set aside a percentage of your income for savings. In addition, consider automatic transfers, so you can stash money away before you get your hands on it.

Spending Habits: Creator of Wealth. Evaluate your habits related to spending money. Did you know that *spending less money* is as valuable as *earning more money*? To look at it another way, spend what's left after saving, instead of saving what's left after spending.

Thirty, Forty, Fifty Years from Now. Let's say that at age 25 you put aside $3,000 a year in a tax-deferred retirement account for ten years and add absolutely nothing else to the account after that. Surprisingly, by the time you reach 65, your $30,000 investment will have grown to just over $472,000, assuming an 8% annual return rate—even though you didn't contribute any more money after age 35.

Here's a different scenario. You could wait until you're 35 to start saving $3,000 a year for thirty years, and you'll have set aside $90,000 of your own money by age 65; yet it will grow to only about $367,000, assuming the same 8% annual rate of return. That's a difference of $105,000 not working in your favor. Save and invest early, and you'll thank yourself later.

In another example, if you were to invest $500 of a windfall each year for the next ten years, your $5,000 investment would be worth nearly $8,000 at the end of that time. If you left that amount to keep growing for another twenty years, you'd have around $25,000, assuming a 6% annual return rate.

How about investing $5 a day? If you invest in an index fund that tracks the market, you could have upwards of $85,000 in 25 years, assuming a 5% annual rate of return. (See the information below about the Acorns app.)

The Only Investment Guide You'll Ever Need by Andrew Tobias is among thousands of books that have been written on investment. For nearly forty years, this particular book has earned the allegiance of more than a million readers across the United States. You may want to join them.

YOU ARE NOT ON SALE.

One day a woman happened to notice that the artist working with a sketchpad in a public place was none other than the world-famous Pablo Picasso. She begged him to draw her portrait. He agreed, worked diligently for one minute, then tore the finished piece from the sketchpad and gave it to her. She loved it—until he told her his fee, which was an astronomical amount. She protested, saying he couldn't possibly ask such a price when he'd taken only a minute to produce the portrait. Picasso's reply was something like, "But you're wrong, *madame*. It took me a lifetime."

Respect the Talent. Artists want to create art. Some of us would execute our craft for free, or even take a financial hit, for the pleasure of doing what we love. Occasionally, performing gratis for the sheer joy of performing, especially for a noble cause, is a good thing—and a great way to acquire recognition. However, working for free on a continual basis undervalues you, the artist, and doesn't honor all the years of training you've invested in developing your skills.

In the case of Mr. Picasso, his swiftly and efficiently created portrait in no way minimized the value of his expertise. It's the value, not the time, that counts. If you wow audiences with your extraordinary technical prowess during your two-minute performance, that brief time in no way negates the 10,000 pliés you've done, or the countless hours, weeks, and years you've spent honing your craft. Proudly submit your invoice.

MO' MONEY.

Active income is money that flows in when you're actively working and stops flowing in when you stop working. Showing up to teach a dance class generates active income. Exchanging time for money and getting paid only when you're working mean that there's a ceiling on how much you can earn in any given 24-hour period.

Passive income is money generated when you aren't actively working, or are putting forth little effort, after the initial development is finished. E-books, software programs, or a dance instructional series that you record once and sell through automated systems all produce passive income.

INVOICE	
Two-minute performance:	$1.00
A lifetime of study to develop the skills to execute said two-minute performance:	$9,999.00
TOTAL	$10,000.00

Residual income is derived from recurring payments and commissions received long after the initial sale is made, usually in specific amounts and at regular intervals. This includes selling goods that are automatically renewable, or consumables that can be automatically reordered.

APPS THAT ARE APT TO BE USEFUL.

It's not all that difficult to figure out how much money comes in and how much needs to go out. If calculating percentages and categorizing isn't something you find enjoyable, try a financial management app like Level Money. It creates a customized budget so that you know how much you can safely spend in a day, a week, or a month, based on your earnings, bills, and savings.

YOUR PLANTS GROW WHEN YOU'RE NOT GIVING THEM YOUR FULL ATTENTION. WHY SHOULDN'T YOUR MONEY DO THE SAME?

Check out these financial management apps.

Digit. Save money by moving some of it from your bank account to your Digit account. Then, you can use that money for something else, such as a trip or a big purchase. The Digit account connects to your bank account and checks your spending habits every day.

Mint. Keep an eye on all your accounts and spending habits so you can learn how to save money. You can create budgets, as well as track and pay bills, while managing your finances, all in one place. Mint even sends you alerts when you need to pay bills.

Good Budget. If you have varying pay schedules, this app is for you because it recreates envelope budgeting, a system in which you put certain amounts of cash into actual envelopes each month. The budget it sets up is based on your cash flow and helps you understand your spending habits.

Pocket Expense. Track spending and get a breakdown of how much you spend per day, week, and month. See what you're spending before you create a budget.

Bill Tracker. This app stores bills and payments, and easily exports your data in a format for Excel, Numbers, or other programs. You can also get alerts to ensure that you make timely payments.

Penny. Using text messaging to explain your income and spending, Penny lets you know when your transactions go through. You can also track spending, upcoming bills, and payments, as well as receive reminders to pay bills.

Acorns. Connect your credit or debit card and checking account to this app. For every transaction, it rounds up the charge to the nearest dollar and invests the difference in a stock portfolio tailored to your age and risk tolerance.

Taking Stock. Don't let the fact that I have an MBA fool you. I learned about buying stocks, diversification, and buy-and-hold strategies the hard way. All my savings were invested in one company, and when it went belly-up, I sat in denial as my $300,000 nest egg disappeared overnight. Like, literally overnight. One minute I was looking at numbers that were black onscreen, and then very quickly those numbers changed to red with minus signs in front of them. Now I understand why no single stock should comprise more than 10% of my stock holdings. Now I know the value of portfolio diversification.

My introduction to credit card use was a disaster. I bought what I wanted when I wanted it. Swiping plastic took the sting out of spending and led me to develop poor money-related habits. Credit card debt was immobilizing and debilitating. It put my life on hold for years. But, I slowly paid off my bills, conducted balance transfers, and bought my way back onto the financial landscape by acquiring a secured card with a low credit limit.

And let's not forget that *the taxman cometh.* A $35,000 gig may result, after taxes, in take-home pay of $27,000. Be aware that with some jobs, you pay your own taxes—so remember to factor in this detail when accepting work.

I've been audited four times. I've cried each time the notice has arrived in the mail. But soon enough, when I'm ready to face reality, I take responsibility for creating whatever situation is at hand and make statements like these: *I'm alive. I love what I do for a living. I'm walking on two legs. I live in a country where I have a sense of freedom and dark chocolate is plentiful.* Then I recall this Ralph Ellison quote: "We look too much to museums. The sun coming up in the morning is enough."

Thinking with gratitude helps me to gain perspective, to remind myself that life is good, and to forgive myself for my past missteps or—in scenarios like the ones just described—my miscalculations. ✦

TELL YOUR MONEY WHERE TO GO INSTEAD OF ASKING WHERE IT WENT.

No Business Like Show Business. When it comes to money, I can count it and that's about it. I hired a financial manager years ago—hands down one of the smartest things I've ever done. I review my monthly statements, and I get a spending allowance. That's right. To this day, I still get an allowance, which is an essential tool that teaches all of us—regardless of where we are in life—how to delay gratification, avoid overspending, save, work for what we want, and work with what we have.

I confess that I didn't start saving until I was 35. Don't follow my lead on that one. Start early! (Another confession: I still count on my fingers, but since I spend my life counting to eight, I have enough fingers.)

Listen, it's called show *business*, and you're not going to have a *show* without first taking care of the *business*, which includes, first and foremost, having good ethics and integrity. Then get out there, do your thing, and pursue your artistic endeavors. If there's one thing I spend too much time thinking about, it's artists dying broke and in obscurity. That's just the saddest thing to me. Debbie Reynolds' business manager ran off with her money years ago, but thankfully Debbie was able to recover and do O.K. for herself. Lesley Gore, the singer of 1960s hits like "It's My Party" and "You Don't Own Me," wasn't as fortunate. At the time of her death, her entire estate was valued at only $50,000. Fred Astaire told the Nicholas Brothers that their performance in *Stormy Weather* was the greatest movie musical sequence he had ever seen, yet Fayard and Harold Nicholas didn't acquire great wealth.

There are so many examples of insolvent artists. This bothers me greatly. Because anyone who spends a lifetime engaging in his or her craft should find a way to be compensated for it. Labors of love deserve compensation, so you may as well get comfortable talking about and accepting money for your craft. It's called show *business* for a reason. Hello! Simple concept. ✦

> I CONFESS THAT I DIDN'T START SAVING UNTIL I WAS 35. DON'T FOLLOW MY LEAD ON THAT ONE. START EARLY!

THE 4-1-1 ON MONEY 101.

Show business is, by its very nature, episodic. One month, or year, or decade, you work nonstop. During the next period, you may work a string of separate and short-lived stints on specific projects and temporary engagements. Seasonal or inconsistent work makes financial management a necessity.

The work that's available today may not be available tomorrow. What worked for your personal brand of excellence yesterday may not work today.

Finance yourself. Take a disciplined approach to money management and invest in the business of you. Take care of your money. And, eventually, your money will take care of you.

20. MIND OVER MANNERS

Aspire to decency. Practice civility toward one another. Admire and emulate ethical behavior wherever you find it. Apply a rigid standard of morality to your lives; and if, periodically, you fail, as you surely will, adjust your lives, not the standards.

~ Ted Koppel

Demonstrating politeness is easy. Most of us have mastered saying *hello, good to see you,* and *I'm looking forward to our next visit.* But what about the interpersonal skills that distinguish you from a robot?

All communication that takes place in relationships—from friendship to romance to the one you have with your dance teacher, agent, or colleague—requires thoughtfulness and tact.

Big Wig. I learned about tact the same day I learned the principal distinction between observing the obvious and speaking it. As an innocent child of ten, I shouted to a neighbor, "I like your new wig!" Her previous wig had been lopsided and her gray hair showed through it. I didn't know that honesty as the best policy has its exclusions. It took me a while to comprehend why my compliment was rude.

Years later, I had another encounter with tact (or the lack of it). While driving home from a Thanksgiving dinner with my brother Kevin, he said, "Remind me never to invite you to go out with me, especially to my friends' home, ever again." I had held court during the dinner. I'd voiced strong opinions about several subjects, including a very negative one about a sitcom the host family loved and had been excited to watch after their holiday meal. My remarks left them speechless, and they scrambled for something else to do instead of watching their favorite show.

I used to involve myself in conversations even though I knew little about the subject. I'd rely only on personal experiences to support my opinions. (Joe Tremaine emailed me this Wayne Dyer quote to include in my story: "The ultimate ignorance is the rejection of something you know nothing about, yet refuse to investigate.") Also, I'm nosy and adventurous. Signs that say *Do not disturb* or *Do not enter* read like invitations to me. I've received my share of attention for my ill-mannered, ill-timed, inappropriate social faux pas. But, fortunately, I'm just as comfortable asking for forgiveness as I am permission.

All my experiences have taught me two incredibly useful and lifesaving doctrines.

If you can't improve the silence, say nothing.

Better to be silent and thought a fool than to speak and remove all doubt. ✦

"THE ULTIMATE IGNORANCE IS THE REJECTION OF SOMETHING YOU KNOW NOTHING ABOUT, YET REFUSE TO INVESTIGATE."

~ Wayne Dyer

FINESSE, FLAIR, AND SAVOIR-FAIRE. CONTROL TIPS:

Think first. Evaluate your words before letting them leave your lips.

Listen to hear. Like really listen.

Show sensitivity when responding to others' opinions so you can make your point without making an opponent. Choose the appropriate time and place to speak. And, say nothing when unclear about what to say, but nod occasionally to indicate that you're engaged.

DANCE TEACHES PROPRIETY.

Dance training produces more than just physical benefits. In dance class, we practice patience while standing attentively with our hands by our sides, waiting our turn during progressions or when another student or group demonstrates. We encourage, support, and applaud fellow dancers as an expression of kindness. We humbly accept corrections with an understanding that learning is a lifelong process. Our silence during class and the asking of permission to enter and exit a class are simply displays of respect for our teachers and fellow dancers. We walk around and never through the middle of a class. We gesture with curtsies, hugs, and handshakes to thank our teachers at the end of class. If we're older or more advanced students, we learn leadership skills through assisting and helping younger dancers.

It's incredible the number of skills you learn during a dance class that will benefit you the rest of your life!

Noting the Obscure. Joe knows he can invite me anywhere and I'll know when to keep my mouth shut, ask a question, take a seat, take the lead, or take my leave. Whether we're visiting a celebrity backstage, fine dining, or conducting a seminar together, diplomacy keeps me in the room or on the invitation list. It may even translate to tangible benefits, such as job offers, higher pay, ideal assignments, promotions, and co-authoring book opportunities. ◆

White-House-Ready. Without manners, you're not going to get too far for too long. I can't think of a single situation in which civility and social graces aren't required—and, might I add, appreciated.

Some people just don't know how to behave. One time I saw a man cross the street without ever looking back to make sure his female companion made it across behind him. He just kept on walking. Several times, I've sat in a theater while parents allowed their young kids to run up and down the aisle like they were at a park. At restaurants I've seen people floss their teeth, lick their fingers, and carry on full-out phone conversations. In fact, once while dining I almost fell out of my chair from witnessing a man cutting his nails at the next table. The woman across from him sat there like it was par for the course.

In 2005, Northwestern University's women's lacrosse team was invited to the White House for a ceremony honoring their NCAA championship. They all thought they were appropriately dressed, but the few who wore bedazzled flip-flops faced controversy and media scrutiny.

This leads to my question: *Are you White-House- or Buckingham-Palace-ready?* If you received an invitation to either of these places, would you know how to carry yourself? And I'm not just talking about which fork to use. You can look that up or pick up clues from someone nearby who knows what they're doing. I'm talking about all the little things: overeating, over-talking, over-drinking, over-sharing, overindulging, or overstaying your welcome... especially at my house. These are the things that count.

Your handshake, demeanor, style of dress, punctuality, and a host of other things—including halitosis and a lack of eye contact—matter. We form opinions about each other. And all it takes is one bad move, one poor choice, in public or private, intentional or otherwise, to tarnish your good name. Whether you like it or not, whether you think it's fair or not, people will make judgments about you that can permanently affect your life and career. And, sad but true, in some instances you may be judged by your worst. If you're not sure what to do, say, or wear, err on the side of caution with a little razzle-dazzle. ✦

IT'S EASIER TO MAKE A GOOD FIRST IMPRESSION THAN APOLOGIZE FOR A POOR ONE.

When Pen Meets Paper, the Words *Thank You* Take on a Whole New Meaning. I'm all about handwritten thank-you notes. I still send them to Joe Tremaine. These little gems are a magical, big gesture—and they don't take that long to write. Recipients appreciate the effort, acknowledge your thoughtfulness, and learn something admirable about you.

Sending a note of gratitude is an expression of appreciation. It makes you stand out as memorable in a good way. Snail mail may be old-fashioned, but old-school will take you places.

I was tired of buying thank-you cards, ten or twenty to a box, and running out. So I printed my own stash and now have a lifetime supply. I chose a timeless photo for the front, included the words "Thank you" on the cover, and put my url, lauriejohnson.com, on the back.

The note itself is a win. Whatever you write inside it makes it that much better. Here's what *I* do. I start with the word *you*, because people love to hear good things about themselves. Next, I mention something specific about the gift or event. Then, toward the end of the note, I express appreciation. I spruce up my cards by signing off with stick figures wearing tap shoes, one of me with my crazy hair, and the other of the person I'm sending the card to. I use speech bubbles to reference something funny between us. Then I add word clouds naming basic tap steps. It's a lot.

WHEN YOU HAVE NOTHING ELSE TO GIVE, GIVE THANKS.

Later, when I see recipients, they thank me for the entertaining thank you, to which I respond, "No, thank *you.*"

When I receive thank-you cards, they go directly in the trash. But not before I make a note of the sentiment by photographing the card's contents and using the pic as the identifying information in my contacts folder.

Often, when I suggest to someone the value of sending notes of gratitude, my listener retorts with something about a lack of time. We all know that's not true. Each of us has time to do whatever it is that we want to do.

Buy a box of thank-you notes and send them in gratitude for gifts you receive. Use them in response to job interviews, letters of recommendation, business lunches, dinner at someone's home, or a rare, infrequent meeting with a mentor whose time you totally appreciate. *Hem your blessings with thankfulness so they don't unravel.* ✦

BE OUR GUEST.

There's not much you can do when you witness people lacking manners, except to note the obvious. Allow us to share with you our own on- and off-the-dance-floor pet peeves. How many of them annoy you as well?

1. Oh, where do I begin? Well, for starters, my name is Joe Tremaine, not Joe. Do not introduce me to anyone as Joe.

2. All somebody's got to do is listen to the lyrics of Cole Porter's "Miss Otis Regrets" or of "Big Spender" from *Sweet Charity* to know that neither song is appropriate content for a kid's routine. Yet I see young dancers performing to these songs all the time. The former is not about a woman with an odd name who's unable to have lunch, and the latter is not about fun, laughs, and good times for kids.

3. I can't stand all this "no problem" in response to "thank you." *No problem* implies that there could have been a problem, but you chose to ignore it (and aren't you a good person for doing so?). Instead, you want to imply that you did whatever it is you're being thanked for because it was your pleasure to do it. Thus, the appropriate response is, "You're welcome."

4. During the end-of-year holidays, some people like to load their greeting cards with glitter or confetti. It spills everywhere. If I see a hint of anything that looks sparkly, it's going in the trash. That stuff gets everywhere and it's not easy to clean up. No one wants an envelope full of glitter.

5. People who discuss politics or religion in mixed company. Look around and pay *attention* to your surroundings.

6. If you get an invitation asking you to RSVP, then *Répondez S'il Vous Plaît.* It's rude to force your host to guess how much food or drink to provide. It's not that difficult to RSVP. Either you're going or you're not.

7. When you visit someone's home, it's customary to bring a modest gift. It doesn't have to be anything big or fancy. Just a little something, something. But I'll tell you what. If you come to my house—invited, of course—don't bring me no big ol' floral bouquet so that I have to stop what I'm doing, find a vase, and rearrange my stuff to accommodate your stuff.

8. If you're talking to me, look at me. Look me in my eyes and speak. And a few *thank yous* never hurt.

9. Speak up. Nobody can read your mind. People will take you seriously only when you say what you mean and mean what you say. Form a sentence and pronounce it clearly. In other words, don't mumble your words. Project.

10. Finally, I don't tolerate intolerance. I don't do bigotry or hatred of any kind. Don't even come near me with it. ◆

> PEOPLE WILL TAKE YOU SERIOUSLY ONLY WHEN YOU SAY WHAT YOU MEAN AND MEAN WHAT YOU SAY.

1. Being interrupted without the offender saying, *"Excusez-moi."*

2. Small-time thinkers. For example, people who, when passing through the first-class cabin while boarding a flight, announce, "Must be nice." Which I interpret to mean, they don't believe it's possible for them to fly first class. Why not upgrade your energy and say or think, "It's just a matter of time before I travel first class" or "I'm first-class. I'm just seated in coach."

3. People who hum or break into song while in a crowd.

4. Kids who disrespect adults, and adults who allow kids to disrespect them.

5. Hearing someone say, "Let's just wait and see what happens" or "I don't want to get involved" or "It's not my place."

6. Dancers who have been with a studio since they were wee tots and then decide to open their own dance school within a few miles of the home studio. Worse still is when they solicit students from the former school or talk trash about their previous or first teachers. I've heard both sides of these stories. There's never a good reason to want to hurt or sabotage another human being.

7. Chronic latecomers who casually assert, "Sorry I'm late." You know they're *not* sorry, because they're *always* late. Lateness is disrespectful.

8. People who spit in public.

9. Dancers who perform onstage with their derrières on display because their leotards or shorts rise up. It's called show business, not show *your* business. ✦

AT THE THEATER.

Laurie: Joe, remember when we were at Radio City Music Hall and we saw those two men wearing T-shirts and baseball caps? Do you think I overreacted when I said their attire disrespected the performing arts and artists?

Joe: Certainly not. I for one don't understand what people are thinking. I mean, come on. If you know you're going to an evening at the theater, the least you can do is change out of beachwear. What's that Karl Lagerfeld quote I like?

Laurie: Oh, I know. "Sweatpants are a sign of defeat. You lost control of your life, so you bought some sweatpants."

Joe: Yes, ma'am. That's the one. Hilarious.

21. CHARACTER MATTERS

Morals are private. Decency is public.

~ Rita Mae Brown

There's a theory that everyone on the planet is separated from everyone else by just six people. In other words, we're all connected to each other through a relatively short chain of acquaintances. If this is true for the world, then it explains why those of us in the dance world know, or know of, each other—and why you don't have to go too far to get someone's take on something or someone in our profession.

Now They're Talking. Your résumé lists the types of work you've done and the directors, producers, and choreographers you've worked for. Some potential employers read your résumé to see what you've done and with whom. They may call each other because, before hiring you, they want to know what it's like to work with you for ten hours a day. They need to get a sense of your appeal, if you have any, and what your attitude is like on set... or anywhere else, for that matter. The issue is, simply, can you get the job done without a whole lot of rigmarole?

I get calls all the time from people asking for recommendations or checking references. Some of them last mere seconds. That's because the slightest hesitation on my end has translated loud and clear to the listener as a "No. Carry on with your search." I don't have to utter a word beyond that and the happy person on the other end says, "Thank you. That's all I needed."

They're happy because they have saved themselves time and money by not hiring someone who might not have the appropriate mindset or skills to act like a professional.

No one is perfect, we all make mistakes, and we all act in different ways. That's normal and that's fine. However, when you manage yourself with discernment, in public and online, you're likely to fare better than people who run wild, with little regard to the impressions they make. You benefit when you carry yourself in such a way that when your name is mentioned, it's followed by upbeat and resounding words and phrases, such as *great, trustworthy, awake, reliable,* and *gets it.* No matter how talented you are as an artist, if you're difficult to work with, I have one word for you: Next! ◆

> NO MATTER HOW TALENTED YOU ARE AS AN ARTIST, IF YOU'RE DIFFICULT TO WORK WITH, I HAVE ONE WORD FOR YOU: NEXT!

GAME OF MOANS.
Being ill-prepared, under-rehearsed, self-absorbed, short-tempered, or viewing others as existing only for one's personal gain are the characteristics of someone who's an annoying liability. The same goes for those who share private conversations, discuss what happened in a closed meeting or rehearsal, or bad-mouth others. Professionals want to work with other professionals. Be the solution.

It's a Small World After All. We all observe, make assessments, and take note of what we see and hear about others. Through social media, glancing at other people's devices to view feeds of their friends, sharing opinions, and everyday, run-of-the-mill *he said, she said,* information trickles and ripples like a game of Telephone. In some instances, the phone call stays live for years because people watch, observe, and remember what you said, how you said it, what you did, and with whom. Your actions can burn bridges, get you on the blacklist, and shut doors, including the front one.

Have Integrity. Profit Forever. Of all the qualities human beings have, integrity is the one I look for first in a person. It's the rock upon which everything is based, and the cornerstone of who you are. It would behoove you not to tell fibs. Because if you do, you'll be known as a liar. And if you gossip... well then, guess what? ✦

REPUTATION: EASIER KEPT THAN RECOVERED.

"If you don't ruin your reputation, you can always get work," noted Bill Murray. A traditional maxim about reputations says that they arrive on foot but leave on horseback. That is, they take years to build yet only seconds to lose. Find your own balance for sharing, commenting, posting, and mixing and mingling. And remember: Your reputation is established with or without your participation.

What's Right vs. What's Easy. Dance styles may come and go, but doing the right thing is forever in style... even when the choice isn't easy, and whether or not anyone is watching. Integrity is the foundation of trust, and with integrity life is simpler. Why? Because doing the right thing and living according to your personal standard of excellence eliminate the need to keep up with any "stories" you may have told previously. When you have nothing to hide, life runs more smoothly. And, best of all, you make it difficult for anyone to malign you.

Reputation Defender. I developed skills of discretion early on because I wanted to be a politician. Since political figures fall under public scrutiny, I began to manage my impulses early on. I still don't post excessive personal content, and can't bring myself to allow a photo to be taken of me with an adult drink in my hand. Someone needs to relax. ✦

IT'S NOT *WHAT* YOU DO. IT'S *HOW* YOU DO WHAT YOU DO.
Life brings with it many things you can't control. A respectable reputation is not one of them.

CHARACTER IS WHO YOU ARE. REPUTATION IS WHAT OTHERS SAY OR THINK YOU ARE.

22. WHO YOU RUN WITH

When the character of a man is not clear to you, look at his friends.

~ Japanese Proverb

The traits of people who spend a lot of time together tend to rub off on each other and, according to a theory, if you average the incomes of the five people you're closest to, the result will be similar to your own income level. Money's not everything—it is, however, something to consider.

No Negative Nothing... Never. I can sense negative people from a distance, the same way I *sense* someone who has over-fragranced (which, by the way, is a pet peeve of mine).

Don't come around me with any kind of negative energy. I ward off negativity to protect my mental state. I control and direct my thoughts toward the positive. I call that my mental armor. I don't let anyone waste my time with their negativity, and I suggest you do the same.

I had a friend I'd lost touch with, and one day I sat down to call her. While dialing the number, I was excited about the conversation we'd have. Then, after (apparently) seeing my name on her caller ID, she answered the phone with "Well, it's about time!" Do you know, I hung up and have never spoken to her again. That's right. I don't deal with negative energy... don't have time for it. ◆

SHOW US WHO YOU RUN WITH, SHOW US WHO YOU ARE.

Human connections influence your attitude and your thoughts. Yet some people spend more time tagging photos or delving into the features of their latest tech devices than they do on their own friendships. Being around a work friend for nine hours a day doesn't mean the connection between the two of you outside of work will necessarily be meaningful. First dates, handshakes, on-the-road driving techniques, and attention to service personnel or others who may go unnoticed... all of these things shed light on who someone is. When communicating—whether online, face to face, or while neighboring or partying—look to a person's code of ethics for clues about who they are and how they do what they do. Connect up. Join forces with people who support you, challenge you, believe in you, and adore you.

THE QUALITY OF YOUR COMPANY ON YOUR JOURNEY IS AS IMPORTANT AS YOUR DESTINATION.

Toxic. Navigating around toxic people used to be a big challenge for me. One day while sitting in the dentist's chair, I had a mini-meltdown between the injection of novocaine and my dentist saying, "Shall we begin?"

I didn't have to go into great detail about my troubles. She gleaned enough information to be able to offer me great advice along with a simple solution.

This is pretty much verbatim what my dentist said to me: "Looka here. There are three kinds of people in this world: growth, neutral, and toxic. You want to hang around your growth people. They're the ones who build you up and make you feel like there's nothing you can't do. They're your cheerleaders, assuring you that the room is better simply because you're in it. I'll say it again—you want to hang out with your growth people." She paused. "Then you have your neutral folks. Like someone you briefly met, for example. Or maybe someone who, when you're out and about, pays you a compliment. If you never saw that person ever again in your life, nothing would change. They're neutral." After another pause and a deep breath she said, "Finally, there's the toxic group. Only one thing to do with these people—limit your interaction with them. Even when they're family members, which is sometimes the case, and which can be difficult."

After years of practice, I've finally mastered managing toxic people and, subsequently, have limited the drama that follows them everywhere they go. I liberated myself. Instead of greeting a toxic person with negativity or a side eye, I initiate a hello with a big, warm smile. I then say something nice about his or her fab shoes, fab hairdo, or general, overall fabulousness. I bid the Toxic One adieu, and make myself scarce. The pleasantries, the compliment, and the ten seconds of small talk diffuse tensions and are constructive substitutes for the truths I really want to speak. This concept of "pushing towards kindness" sounded incredibly counterproductive to me at first. Where I grew up, if someone did something to you, you got them back, and you upped the game.

Suppressing opinions feels fake, but giving someone a piece of your mind ... where's that going to get you except a bit of short-term satisfaction? You can't change anyone, so go ahead and lead and set a good example.

Kindness gets easier with practice. And, if someone thinks you're a wimp for choosing love over other options, they have no idea how powerful a feeling it is to walk away knowing you ran the show. Stay on your mission. Those who direct energy towards pettiness waste time. If you don't want to create a situation, don't create a situation. ✦

> YOU CAN'T CHANGE ANYONE, SO GO AHEAD AND LEAD AND SET A GOOD EXAMPLE.

Hollywood Connection. I moved from New York to Los Angeles after landing a great job with Jerry Lewis, who at the time was one of the top stars in the world. He took me under his wing and showed an interest in my career. He introduced me to everybody who was somebody, and over the years I've worked to maintain those contacts.

I branched out further and connected with a group of ladies called SHARE. Seven women, over a lunch date back in 1953, created this group to serve disabled and abused children. Their tagline is "Share Happily and Reap Endlessly," and today they've raised over $48 million for these kids and for medical research.

Networking and maintaining my connections is by far one of the best things I've ever done. You can't go wrong by reaching out and saying, "Hello." You have to start somewhere and "hello" is as good a start as any. ✦

SECTION 5

HELP AND INSPIRATION

23. FINDING YOUR MENTORS

The best teachers are those who show you where to look,
but don't tell you what to see.

~ Alexandra K. Trenfor

Some people excel beyond what they initially thought possible because *someone else thought they could.* That "some-one" in many cases is a mentor. Sometimes mentors are people with whom you already have some connection. You may have mentors yet call them mom, coach, auntie, guidance counselor, or fav dance teacher.

Supporting Cast. I have three mentors who are with me all the time and who guide my actions: Broadway icon Chita Rivera, June Taylor of the June Taylor Dancers, and Mr. Clarke Williams, a community leader from my small hometown in Louisiana.

No matter what's going on in my life, I call upon the wisdom of these three individuals to keep me on the straight and narrow. I've been using this technique for years, and it works wonders. Through them, I activate my own inner guidance system of checks and balances to do what's right. I ask questions like these: *Would I let them see me in this situation? What would they think about me creating this choreography? Would they be proud of me for the choices I'm making? What would they do in my current predicament?*

They each inspire me in different ways. Chita always says, "Joe, I've got 20 minutes left." That's her way of reminding me to use my time here on earth as best I can. June Taylor was someone I admired for her innovative work in dance. Clarke Williams taught me that good guys can and do finish first. He was chairman of CenturyTel, Inc., a huge communications company. He'd say to me, "Joe Wayne, I'm going to be watching you when you leave Louisiana and head for New York. I expect great things."

Each of these people trusted me to live up to a particular standard, and their trust has served as my motivation. That's a beautiful thing. ✦

> I HAVE THREE MENTORS WHO ARE WITH ME ALL THE TIME AND WHO GUIDE MY ACTIONS.

Facetime. I've not had face-to-face time with a lot of my mentors but I know their tweets, interviews, blogs, or keynote presentations. Question: What do Gary Vaynerchuk, Eric Thomas, Harriett Tubman, and Eleanor Roosevelt have in common? Not much other than the fact that they are four people I like. I've not met T.D. Jakes, Ester Hicks, Michael Bernard Beckwith, Marianne Williamson, Lisa Nichols, Wayne Dyer, Zig Ziglar, Jim Rohn, Dale Carnegie, or any other thought leader whose quotes open this book's chapters. But their brand of inspiration and guidance appeals to my sensibilities. I love that mentorship isn't limited by time or proximity.

Consider subscribing to *Success Magazine* to leverage your success. In addition to great articles, each issue includes an audio CD, the content of which is priceless. Get your copy today. ✦

FINDING A MENTOR.

Mentorships are informal, not contractual, relationships. There's no need to directly ask someone to mentor you, or to wait for someone to choose you. Rather, make a connection with the individual who's doing what you want to do or has been where you want to go. Look for somebody you respect personally and appreciate professionally, someone who embodies the characteristics you admire. Once you find people you like, study their work, words, and actions. Deepen your awareness and knowledge further by studying *the person who inspired your mentor*. Allow the relationship to grow naturally—as you would any other. If the person is a good match for you (and you a good match for the prospective mentor), he or she will respond with equal interest.

Mentors provide support for and guidance on all kinds of areas. Some business and mentor relationships evolve to include personal matters. Be smart about what you share with individuals you do not know well or with whom you have not yet developed trust and rapport. Value your privacy while getting acquainted with a mentor. Keep knowing every little detail about you as an earned *privilege*.-

OBSERVE THE MISSTEPS OR TRIUMPHS OF OTHERS AND ADD YOUR OWN WISDOM TO WHAT YOU SEE. YOU ARE YOUR GREATEST TEACHER.

24. WHAT I WISH I HAD KNOWN

Many receive advice; only the wise profit from it.

~ Harper Lee

We asked our friends, colleagues, and contemporaries to reflect upon their careers and to answer this question: *What do you wish you had known or wish someone had told you when you were just beginning your show biz career?* We got an earful, so open yours wide.

"I wish I'd known how long a career could actually last. Then I might not have been so worried about having such a late start."

– Director, Choreographer

"Someone once said to me, 'How is a person to know if you don't tell them?'—meaning, if you see an opportunity, a job, or something you want to explore, don't be afraid to speak up to those who can mentor you, or help you achieve your goal."

– Entertainment Producer

"There's going to be a time when your art will become a business. I wish I'd known beforehand how to navigate that. I did it through trial and error. This how-to book that Laurie and Joe have written is so good... Watch people who have become great at what they do and who know how to behave. So much of show business is how you behave. Will people want to work with you? Will people like you? How you behave is such a big part of everything."

– Director, Producer, Choreographer, Dancer

"Do whatever you have to do in order to earn a living in a way that represents the business you've chosen. Teach kids instead of waiting tables. Choreograph for middle school and high school musicals instead of standing behind a cash register. You never know where you'll meet the next opportunity... Learn as much as you can with your body and your mind. Look at yourself as two entities: 'Me' and 'Me, Inc.'... At the point of being a professional dancer, you are a product. If the producer wants a Coke and you're a Pepsi, no matter how good you are, you're just not what the producer wants. It has no reflection on your ability or your talent or your being. It's a business. Treat it that way."

– Master Teacher, Entrepreneur, Producer, Director

"I wish someone had told me to humbly publicize my successes so I could have extended my longevity as a dancer or choreographer in this business."

– Director, Choreographer

"Stay true to your talent and gifts. If you're not in the 'in crowd' or an 'A list' dancer, don't worry about it! You're a dancer and an artist. Whether you're on the Academy Awards, a world tour, a popular video or TV show, or if you're performing in Las Vegas, Tahoe, Branson, New York, or on a cruise ship—you're making a living doing what you love. Enjoy each and every moment. And when you look back on your career, you'll remember the sense of accomplishment, self-satisfaction, and joy produced by having actually worked in an incredible arena called dance… On the road to fulfilling your dance goals, take pride in each step of 'the journey.' From the classroom to the stage, always be grateful that you can create, you can move, you can express, you can choose, you can feel, you can participate, you can influence, you can make someone think, you can dance!"

– Master Teacher, Entrepreneur, Producer, Director

"The dance classroom: many answers, discoveries, preparations, and opportunities are found there. Study, study, study. Time and time again I've witnessed this. The way one takes class is the way one rehearses, is the way one performs. There's a clear through-line. The integrity of the performer is cultivated in the classroom. It doesn't happen once you get the job. It was happening all along the way. It's an exciting way to enter the classroom—filled with your own potential to learn more and more. Great artists and visionaries embark on a never-ending quest to learn, and it all starts in class."

– Choreographer, Dancer, Teacher, Director, Producer

"Thinking I knew so much. But the reality was that I needed to learn a whole lot more…
Also, the value of having business savvy."

– Producer, Publisher

"Back then, we didn't think about building a career in entertainment. It happened naturally. You got a lucky break, and you did what you had to do to stay in it so you could keep doing what you love to do."

– Beloved Actress of Theater, Television, and Film

"I wish someone had informed me that I would have to wear a dance belt throughout my dance life. Really? I'm still not about wearing it, but they *are* a necessity."

– Performer, Actor, Singer-Songwriter, Artist, Company Co-Founder

"I never knew it would be so crowded in the elevator headed up to the top floor."

– Award-Winning Choreographer

"I was always told by my mom that I was the best. But you think parents say that just because they have to. I wish I would have realized as a young boy that no matter how many dancers are out there, no one is exactly like you. So take what makes you individual and amplify it! Being yourself, magnified, is the best way to find success and longevity."

– Producer, Director, Choreographer, Fashion Designer, Entrepreneur

"A career is built upon the opportunities that don't go your way. Keep your eyes and ears open, move forward with confidence, and never ever lose your sense of humor."

– Director, Choreographer, Educator

"That talent is only one third of what is required for success. The other two thirds are people skills and business skills."

– Dancer, Actor, Comedian, Entertainer

"If I knew how much dance was going to break my body, I would have taken better care of it. I would have been more careful about creating movement that was more nourishing to the body."

– Creator, Director, Choreographer

"Being yourself is good enough."

– Choreographer, Teacher, Dancer

"Like many things, you have to learn by doing—or even to learn the hard way. When I moved to LA, I had a misconception that you needed to 'create a look' for yourself. There *is* some truth to this statement. But I was told that an extreme look is key. Now *that* is wrong! Having blue hair and shaved sides is NOT going to book you on every gig. (Yet for some people it works and it's their signature because that's who they are truly. Rock on! Amazing.) Also remember that having an extreme look will box you in to certain types of roles from a casting perspective. If the look is true to you and who you are, then do it! (After all, what is life without living and loving the honest you anyway?!) The moral of the story is that being true to YOU is indeed YOUR LOOK. At the end of the day, casting needs one of everything!! Tall, short, dark hair, light hair, skin colors, all the people of the rainbow. Every gig varies as to what is needed. So be you and be only you. In Hollywood, there will be plenty of others with your look, skill level, etc. So make sure that when a look-alike of you comes along, there's no competition of who wore you better. #booked"

– Artist, Dancer, Choreographer

"It's O.K. to ask questions. If you really don't know what the protocol is, ask. Use your resources and don't be afraid to ask questions."

– Dancer, Choreographer, Teacher

"Find a good balance in your life for staying focused and motivated. I feel that you work so hard trying to make it that you don't give yourself downtime to enjoy friends and other pleasures. On the other hand, because everyone is on their own schedule it could also be easy for some dancers to become lazy and not as productive as they should be. Self-motivation is the key. Finding that balance is so important."

– Commercial Artist, Dancer, Convention Teacher

"I wish I'd known that intangibles besides talent make you successful."

– Choreographer, Company Founder

"Communication and humble confidence are key elements that work in conjunction with technique, tenacity, and being a team player. Dance is graceful; communication within the industry should have the same approach... The secret to the dance industry is recognizing that your love of dance is a gift."

– Dance Agent, Commercial Dance Educator

"No matter how talented or ambitious you might be at that moment, you could be passed over just because you don't fit the part. Sometimes it's just not your time. Don't make the disappointment personal."

– Author, Speaker, Beauty and Image Expert

"The one thing I wish I had known is to just do it. Trust yourself and take action."

– Dancer, Producer, Choreographer, Writer

"I wish someone would have explained to me the importance of being your own advocate in this business. I kept waiting for 'someone else' to tell me I was talented enough, or even merely good enough, to ask for what I wanted. I truly feel I would have been bolder with my choices in my career in this industry had I known that."

– Master Teacher, Choreographer

"I skated first, then I built a love for music and dance. I wish I'd learned to dance sooner."

– Dance Industry Veteran

"I wish I knew more about music so that I could speak to musicians in the language they understand. As dancers, we count in 8's if the music is in 4/4 time. Musicians count in bars that are only 4 beats in 4/4 time. I also didn't know that a blues chorus was 12 bars and a standard song form chorus was 32 bars. As a tap dancer working with live musicians, you need to know these things."

– Dancer, Choreographer

"I wish I'd had knowledge about the financial side of the dance industry: what dancers make, yearly income ranges, what it takes to make a living, etc. I also knew nothing about unions, dues, residuals, eligibility requirements, or how unions and support groups advocate for us. There are benefits available, and taking advantage of what those groups have to offer would have been great."

– Director, Choreographer, Dancer, Producer

"To stay focused on my path and not worry about what anyone else was doing."

– Choreographer, Master Instructor

"Don't be afraid to have your own voice and style. Don't follow the trend—create your own."

– Performer, Choreographer

"I wish someone had told me to do more research on the choreographers and what they're looking for. Research pays off abundantly. In my day it wasn't as necessary. But in today's market it's a must."

– Dancer, Teacher, Musician, Choreographer

"I wish someone had told me that I could actually do this as a career, that I could travel the world and teach anywhere—with the right connections. I didn't know how small a world the dance industry is."

– Dancer, Choreographer, Teacher, Actor

"When learning dance, you start with your brain, then you put in your heart. Then you let it go and just give it up to your higher power. Then it's all good whatever happens."

– Beloved Dance Convention Teacher

"I wish I'd known more about the business side when I first moved to Los Angeles. I wish I'd listened to everyone when they warned me to save money. I wish I'd realized I might need a backup plan if I got hurt. I wanted to do a Broadway show, so I wish I'd given more attention to my voice lessons. I wish I'd have been more outgoing when I was younger."

– Dancer, Choreographer, Teacher, Talent Agent

"It isn't in MY control. That's what I wish I had understood when I was first starting my career. Simple, right? So simple, in fact, that it's hard to realize the full capacity of this expression. Many times I want to book whatever audition I'm on. If I didn't I wouldn't be there, right? Wrong. Sometimes I go to an audition because I ACTUALLY want the job, and sometimes I go to please my agents, or because there's been a lack of auditions, or because there's nothing else going on, so... why not? Once I get there I find myself in the pool of competition and now I want to WIN. So, you see, it isn't about booking the audition because it's a job or project that I care about—it's about winning the offer. I put myself on the line and I want validation. I give up my power as the artist because now it's about the ego and, essentially, I care about things that ARE NOT IN MY CONTROL. It's not about the craft and doing my best from a place of love. What it becomes is that I want to do my best because I want my ego to be stroked; therefore, my performance will probably suffer in some way. Maybe I won't be free, or maybe I didn't take risks I otherwise would have if I'd operated from my heart and not my head. When it comes to artistry, the only thing you can control is what you do. That's it. Literally everything else is up to someone or something else. The variables in the entertainment industry are ENDLESS. Those reasons can be petty and also valid. Either way, it doesn't matter! All you can control is what YOU do."

– Actor, Teacher, Dancer

"Study more ballet."

– Choreographer, Dance Convention Administration Director

"Looking back, I realize that the answers were in the journey. There were so many mentors and things along the way that changed the journey—and there still are. I could say I wish someone had told me to listen more, or focus or practice more, or be more passionate, or have more fun on the journey, or follow my heart, or learn to be in touch with my higher self. I'm sure someone did tell me all of those things. But I was probably too young or not far enough into the journey to hear. . . .Today I find that mentally I need to be passionate about my thoughts. But I don't think that's something you can teach. Chita Rivera's solo debut performance at 84 years of age at Carnegie Hall on November 7, 2016, showcased this: The secret to life is to enjoy the journey. The problem with youth—anyone under 60—is that they think they hear, but it's really only a surface hearing. They don't yet have enough experience to comprehend the depth of the layers of insight or advice. When I was younger, I was told everything that I was capable of assimilating. Now I ask myself, 'Why didn't I know who I was—and know that I was capable of accomplishing anything I wanted?' My cultural and religious background was one of limitation, not optimism. No one knew any better. I loved the performing arts, but no one knew what that was and there was no guidance. I had to do it on my own—that was my journey. Not having guidance was the journey."

– Dance Convention Owner, Producer

"It's been a journey, and getting lost is part of the journey. Every day I feel like I'm just getting started, like I'm just warming up."

– Director

"Perform on each dance job as if it's the only one you'll ever have. Savor every opportunity to work with a new teacher or choreographer, because you'll learn something from each of them. Perform longer before you become a teacher or choreographer, because experience gives you a deeper well to draw from as a creator and teacher."

– Dancer, Choreographer, Master Teacher

"That I was good enough even when I didn't get the job. Getting cut has nothing to do with my dancing. I'm just not the right look. *You're a blond and we want a brunette.* Sometimes it's that simple."

– Professional Dancer, Teacher, Choreographer

"I wish someone had told me how much my love for dance would consume me. It came as a total surprise. I just wanted to dance."

– Dance Convention Director

"Tap dancing is an essential skill. It teaches balance, patience, syncopation, timing, coordination, rhythm, and so much more. You can stay together with the group when you have a background in tap. Still, I wish I'd known how to keep my mouth shut just a little bit more. Sometimes."

– Choreographer

"I wish I'd known the following: **1.** Not everyone is going to want to see you succeed, even those you consider close friends. **2.** It's going to take at least a year to really get an idea of what this industry is like. Commit. **3.** Having popularity on social media, or a few random gigs, is not a career. It's an experience. **4.** Friendships come and go quickly; but when you find the right people for you, appreciate them. **5.** Your persona to strangers on social media should not be more important than the actual relationships you have with friends and family. **6.** Laugh more. It's cute to think every setback defines your life, but we know this isn't true. **7.** Your time is valuable. Value your time. **8.** Don't drive in LA between the hours of 5 a.m. and 11 p.m. unless you want a slight headache."

– Professional Dancer, Choreographer

"I wish I'd known that I didn't need to be perfect. My teacher instilled in us that we were never good enough. Live audiences get to see the show one time, and you cheated them if you weren't on it that night. But I took it to an extreme and was too hard on myself."

– Dancer, Choreographer, Director

"Early on in a dancer's professional career, she or he is faced with a decision to choose a path. One path will be a wild ride of exciting, somewhat risky, and even dangerous jobs that compromise the body over and over again and lead to a short 'flash in the pan' career. Or, on a different path, you can opt for longevity, with a career a bit more wisely chosen and more conservative, but one that can still be amazingly rewarding and fulfilling—a career in which you still keep the body whole and dancing forever. The dancer will have to decide one way or the other. I encourage the dancer to think about this and make a conscious decision rather than have it be made for them."

– Dancer, Choreographer, Teacher

"**1.** You may be the best dancer in the room and the choreographer may love you, but there are some jobs where that doesn't matter. It may all come down to who the producer or the 'star' determines is best suited for the part. **2.** Surprisingly, some choreographers or directors may shy away from hiring you if they feel intimidated or threatened by your talent, or fear you could outshine them in their own field. It's sad but true. The ego of some people is a strong, powerful thing, and their insecurities get in their way. **3.** If you're wanting to be in the Broadway world and you see yourself as primarily a dancer, start training your singing and vocal skills. If it comes down to you being one of the final three dancers up for a job, in many cases casting directors will hire the strongest singer in the room—NOT necessarily the strongest dancer. But don't let that scare you! Overcome any fears you may have about singing. Master a few good audition songs, and it could pay off wonderfully! **4.** If you want to be in a dance company, that may be some of the hardest dancing you'll do as a professional, and you may spend time as an unpaid apprentice. It can take years to make a living in a company because many of them have tight budgets. Company work is really rewarding, just with smaller pay scales compared to some other gigs. **5.** As dancers, we're always told that it's key to be versatile, to be a chameleon, to do it all. That's great—and very true. Remember that the commercial world, the film world, and the Broadway world are not going anywhere. So if you want to try to achieve a job in all of those arenas, plan it out accordingly based on the longevity of your body, what jobs you'll be right for at what age, and where you want to live."

– Dancer, Teacher, Choreographer

"Don't expose your weakness; only show your strengths. In the words of Toni Basil: *Act seasoned.*"

– Professional Dance Choreographer, Teacher

"Stay loyal. Often the opportunity is right in front of you, but you can't see it if you're looking for the bigger job with the bigger pay. Stay loyal to the people who bring you up. They came into your life for a reason."

– Choreographer, Dancer

"In life and in show business, it's about building relationships—not just friendships. If you're not nice, fun, or a good person, you're not going to work. Look to create win-wins. Instead of *What can he or she give me?*, think *What can I do for this person? Can I bring her (or him) a coffee? Thousands of people want the same job, so how can I stand out? What's going to make me memorable? Where's the win-win?* Life isn't about taking. Taking isn't going to win relationships... Kenny Ortega set a nurturing tone when I worked with him. He said to me, 'Don't ever say you messed up.' This was a valuable dance lesson and life lesson."

– Entertainment Host, Reporter

"I wished my early dance education included greater information and guidance as to how to protect my body (ankles, knees, neck, and back) from sustaining injury that could create irreversible damage. I danced as if my body would be forever invincible."

– Producer, Director, Choreographer

"To learn how to separate yourself from what you're selling."

– Dancer, Choreographer, Philanthropist

"I wish I had known how much I would love show business. I've never fallen out of love with it."

– Actress, Author, Broadway Veteran, Philanthropist

"Keep yourself the way you are. Remember your roots and your foundation. Don't forget who you are—because it's easy to give up your soul for dance."

– Dancer, Choreographer

"Become the leader of your own life. People who become great don't fear. The bold succeed. Be soulful, funky, and have a good time."

– Choreographer, Director, Editor

"There are lots of ups and downs, so don't get a false sense of comfort. Don't get complacent and think you reached that level."

– Dancer, Choreographer, Artistic Director

"That my friends would become my family... I wish I'd known that the aggression inside me was going to stay with me forever, because I would have been nicer sooner. I didn't need to act out when I was younger."

– Dancer, Choreographer, Visual Architect

"This industry is a business. You can make your passion and love for dance into a career, but just remember: *The dance world is a business.* Show up. Blend in. Hustle."

– Choreographer, Dance Convention Teacher

"Keep your eyes open out there. You can go from dancing to so many other careers. Dance takes you places."

– Actor, Musician, Singer, Songwriter, Producer, Filmmaker

"I wish someone had told me to simply be myself. Because I spent the first number of years just trying to figure out how to smile, what shoes to wear, how to act, etc. You have to know yourself and know your ideas for yourself."

– Choreographer, Artistic Director, Producer

"It's not about being friends with the in-crowd. It's about being the best... *your* best."

– Costume Designer, Dancer

"Take singing lessons so you can carry a tune... And don't compare your success to the success of others."

– Choreographer, Dancer, Teacher

"I wish I'd trusted myself sooner to be myself—rather than trying to be or look like someone else in my early career."

– Dancer, Choreographer, Instructor

"I wish I had known how powerful identity is. Knowing yourself is a process, so don't lose yourself in the process. This business is always about business."

– Actor, Producer, Husband, Dad

"You can inherently be yourself and succeed. It doesn't matter if you're white, straight, muscular, or whatever. Stay true to yourself and own yourself up and down. There will be days when you feel like you don't fit in, but those are your best days."

– Choreographer, Dancer, Educator, Consultant

"I would love to have known that every journey is vastly different... and that you should try not to compare yourself to others' success—because it can be deadly. Trust your own path."

– Teacher, Choreographer, Theater and Television Performer

"I wish someone had told me to brand myself earlier in my career. As dancers we're commodities, so it's important to see yourself that way."

– Choreographer, Teacher

"No matter how hard you work on Broadway or in a company, you may not get to the top. Make your own career, and make opportunities for yourself. It's risky and possible. If you work hard, you can achieve greatness in any area."

– Creative Director, Choreographer

"Make sure that what you do, you're doing it for you and not for someone else or some company that wants to use you for your popularity. Make sure you trust and know who you're working with."

– Dancer

"I took things personally. Because when you invest your heart in something and it doesn't work out, it's upsetting. Don't get so upset. Trust in what's meant to be and go with that. Don't stress."

– Singer, Songwriter, Dancer, Choreographer

"Keep your inner circle small and your networking circle big. Not everyone you work with is going to be your best friend."

– Artist, Husband, Father, Son, Brother

"I've been dancing since I was two-and-a-half, and I'm still performing and dancing. Sometimes 12 hours on sets. And at my age. I love it... I wish I had taken care of my early injuries and not always danced through them. Be kind to your body and listen to it. If you have an injury, rest and do physical therapy. By doing this, you'll have a longer career in what you love: dancing."

– Entertainment Veteran

"You're perfect the way you are. Just be yourself."

– Dancer, Choreographer

"I wish someone had told me how to navigate show biz once I had the dance chops. There's so much more to it than just dance. The operative word is BUSINESS. Dancers need to know more about the business side of show biz."

– Master Teacher, Choreographer, Associate Professor

"I wish I could do it all over again. I wish I had known how good I was—but yet, I still don't know. Still today at 84 years old, I meet with directors and pray to God I can interpret what they want. I'm scared, yet at the same time I'm saying, 'Let me at it.'"

– Dancer, Singer, Actress, Broadway Star

THANKS TO ALL THE DANCE EDUCATORS, ICONS, ZENITHS, AND VISIONARIES WHO STRENGTHEN OUR INDUSTRY, AND MAKE THE LANDSCAPE OF THE WORLD MORE BEAUTIFUL.

25. IN CASE YOU DIDN'T KNOW

We are not makers of history. We are made by history.

~ Martin Luther King, Jr.

Imagine you're an expert, a professional, in some fancy industry whose history is so rich and interesting that you've become passionate about it. A person approaches you announcing that she's also a professional and also loves the very thing you love. You get to chatting with her, and all is right with the world—that is, until you casually mention a basic, well-known fact about the history of this industry you both love, and she's clueless.

Initially, you're forgiving. You don't expect everyone to know every historical fact and detail about what they claim to have a passion for. But, as the conversation continues and it becomes obvious that this fellow aficionado has no historical context or point of reference, you become a little perplexed—and just a tinge annoyed. After all, she referred to herself as a professional. Please!

GAIN A PERSPECTIVE THAT ONLY HISTORY CAN IMPART.

History tells the story of how we got to where we are. One part of being in show business is knowing, at least to some degree, about the greats who helped shape and define the arts and entertainment history. Researching and enhancing your understanding of what they did and how they shared their talents is *important*. Looking back at similarities and differences in how past individuals did what you do today can show you what's possible ahead. And, if by chance you're currently not inspired to do such researching and enhancing for yourself, then do it in gratitude for those whose shoulders you have the luxury and privilege of dancing upon.

This chapter helps you get started. Here, you'll discover questions and answers that cover historical and contemporary facts and details about dance. Because comprehensive information, historical and otherwise, would require volumes (the origins of our art form run deep!), what we've included can be considered broad, random strokes in twelve categories.

HISTORY MATTERS.

Moves, Grooves, Styles, and Steps 117
A Place for Dance 118
Take Me to the Ballet 118
As Seen on TV 119
All the World's a Stage 120
The Silver Screen 120

Names to Know 121
Lingo 123
Jazz Gypsies 123
Anything Goes 125
Tap-able Tap-tations 125
Iconic Videos 126

Did you know that the word *history* comes from a Greek word meaning "investigation"? If any of our facts or details sound interesting or spark your curiosity, check them out. Investigate. Find out what all the talk is about.

1. MOVES, GROOVES, STYLES, AND STEPS

This dance, named after a South Carolina city, was prevalent in the early 1900s and popularized ragtime jazz music.
Charleston

Lord of the Dance popularized this type of dance.
Irish step dancing

A style of dance that evolved outside of a studio setting and includes locking, popping, breaking, Chicago footworking, juking, house dance, tutting, roboting, and krumping.
Street dance

Bruce Lee is known professionally as a martial artist, philosopher, filmmaker, and holder of the 1958 Hong Kong championship in this style.
Cha-cha

The Rock Steady Crew, a street crew created in 1977 by Bronx B-boys Jimmy D and Jimmy Lee which became home to Richard Colón (better known by his stage name, Crazy Legs), are known as the fathers of this dance form.
Breakdancing

The goal of this dance, which originated in Trinidad and became very popular at beach parties in the '60s, was to see how low one can go.
Limbo

Radio City's legendary dance company, The Rockettes, formerly known as the Missouri Rockettes, holds rigorous auditions in which dancers must be proficient in these three styles of dance.
Jazz, ballet, and tap

Athletic prowess blends with artistic expression in this Brazilian martial arts form incorporating jumps, flips, turns, and lunges to music.
Capoeira

Girls wearing long skirts, voluminous petticoats, and black tights perform this high kicking dance, usually in Parisian music halls.
Can-Can

The street term for this step is the Backslide. Michael Jackson popularized it during his Motown 25th Anniversary performance.
Moonwalk

This food is also the name of a popular rock and roll dance from the 1960s.
Mashed Potato

What lyrical is to ballet, with the feet turned out, this style is to modern, with the feet more often in parallel.
Contemporary

This foot-shuffling, pelvis-twisting dance, inspired by African-American plantation workers, has its origins in the 1890s. It was also a popular song in the 1960s.
The Twist

This step, also known as a Helicopter, is not your regular cup of joe.
The Coffee Grinder

This version of the fox trot, comprised of extremely quick stepping and syncopated foot patterns, is considered among the most difficult of all the ballroom dances.
Quick Step

The Spanish name of this dramatic ballroom style requiring both acting and dancing skills translates as "double step."
J Paso Doble

The Paso Doble, which draws on the tradition of bullfighting, is a theatrical dance in which the man is characterized as the matador and the woman is said to be what?
The bullfighter's cloak or cape

2. A PLACE FOR DANCE

This East Coast drop-in studio, established in the 1980s, offers over fifty classes each day, as well as professional, children's, teen, and Visa programs.

Broadway Dance Center

Founded in 1992 in the NOHO (North Hollywood) Arts District by two dancers who met in Frank Hatchett's class at Broadway Dance Center, this studio is referred to as "the place where it all happens." It is a global brand with locations around the world and a philosophy of "Unity in Diversity."

Millennium Dance Complex

In 1979, this *Singin' In the Rain* actor and dancer opened her own dance studio, which bears her name, in North Hollywood, CA. It's where Michael Jackson rehearsed for his "Thriller" music video.

Debbie Reynolds Dance Studios

This popular Massachusetts dance festival unites artists from different countries and of all ages, and gives them an opportunity to train with multiple master choreographers. It showcases hundreds of performances from some of the most prestigious dance companies in the U.S.

Jacob's Pillow Dance Festival

This global company is one of the world's leading producers and providers of family entertainment in film and in parks, and employs dancers, actors, and other creative artists as cast members in over forty countries.

The Walt Disney Company

One of the largest theatrical producers in the world and leader in circus arts and street entertainment, this company holds residencies all over the U.S., but especially in Las Vegas, and employs more than 1,000 dancers annually.

Cirque de Soleil

Founded in 1979, this studio is the epicenter of New York's professional dance community, offering classes seven days a week, for all ages, taught by internationally recognized artists and teachers.

Steps on Broadway

3. TAKE ME TO THE BALLET

A ballet enthusiast is called this.

Balletomane

Vaganova, Cecchetti, Royal Academy of Dance (RAD), Ballet School of the Opéra National de Paris, Balanchine, and Bournonville are names of these.

Ballet training systems

This ballet company, the world's largest with over 240 dancers, was founded in Moscow in 1776. Its Russian name translates as "big, large, great, or important."

Bolshoi

Created by a ballet dancer whose first name is Joseph, this training method designed to strengthen core muscles is known by his last name.

Pilates

Many dance companies like Ballet Boyz, Dance Theatre of Harlem, and Alvin Ailey American Dance Theater bring innovation to dance. This New-York-based ballet company is no different. They fuse together classical ballet, Latin, and contemporary dance, and celebrate their Latino culture.

Ballet Hispanico

A principal male ballet dancer is referred to as this.

Danseur noble, the masculine equivalent to prima ballerina

He ignited the popularity of men in ballet and was referred to as the greatest male dancer of the early 20th century. He was celebrated for his seemingly gravity-defying leaps, and his ability to dance en pointe.

Vaslav Nijinsky

World renowned for his television, stage, and film performances, this Russian ballet dancer took the traditionally supporting role of the male dancer to a new level by combining classical ballet and modern dance. In his own productions, he created more choreography for men, and his influence on the world of ballet changed the perception of male dancers.

Rudolf Nureyev

Known for his impressionist style of painting, this artist's interest in the human physique drew him into the world of ballet; the majority of his paintings, sculptures, and sketches are of ballet dancers.

Edgar Degas

Ballets such as *Don Quixote, Cinderella, Swan Lake, A Midsummer's Night Dream, Sleeping Beauty, and Alice in Wonderland* were adapted from folk stories and these.

Fairy tales

This Tchaikovsky composition was unsuccessful after its first year because people thought the music was too difficult to dance to. After Tchaikovsky's death, however, the piece was revived and is now oh, so popular.

Swan Lake

We don't melt cheese or chocolate in ballet class, but we do this.

Fondu

The English translations of plié, tendu, and chassé are

Bend, stretch, and chase

Dance goes toe to toe with sports as some athletes take ballet to improve their timing, range of motion, and balance. You may notice traces of a pas de chat in a soccer player's footwork, a chassé before a baseball shortstop throws the ball, and this, performed in parallel second position as a basketball player prepares at the free throw line.

Plié

Former Pittsburgh Steeler wide receiver Lynn Swann says his ballet training enhanced his athletic skills, and his Hall of Fame citation referenced his "fluid movements" and "tremendous leaping ability." A sportscaster once referred to him as "the Baryshnikov of" this.

Football

4. AS SEEN ON TV

Ed McMahon hosted this reality television show, which helped launch the careers of Britney, Christina, Usher, and NSYNC. Many dancers and choreographers, including Jackie Sleight, who choreographed a win for her groups A Sleight Touch and Boys Club, were featured performers.

Star Search

Before the age of "reality television," entertainment was enjoyed on these types of shows hosted by Ed Sullivan, Carol Burnett, and Lawrence Welk, to name a few.

Variety shows

Dick Clark, referred to as "America's oldest teenager," hosted this popular show featuring dancing teenagers, beginning in the 1950s. The show piqued worldwide interest in dance and pop culture for over five decades.

American Bandstand

For more than thirty years, Don Cornelius hosted this show, referred to as the "hippest trip in America." It became a cultural phenomenon, launching the careers of popular artists and leading the way for the latest music, culture, art, fashion, and, of course, dance moves.

Soul Train

This show, hosted by Rick Dees and Arsenio Hall, debuted in 1980 and counted down the Top 10 chart hits of the week. Each week a troupe of eight danced the choreography of Anita Mann, Lester Wilson, and Kevin Carlisle, to name a few.

Solid Gold

5. ALL THE WORLD'S A STAGE

This type of stage, with its upstage end higher than its downstage end, makes the performance easier to see and improves the view for the audience, regardless of where in the house they may sit.

Raked stage

A stage is a three-sided box; the name of the "wall" through which the audience sees the action is called this.

The fourth wall

These direct the blocking of scenes and actor entrances and exits, and communicate to performers where to focus or to travel.

Stage directions

When you're onstage facing the audience, "corner one" is here.

Downstage to your right

The color of this backstage waiting room is attributed to the nausea some performers feel before going onstage, given that the color is supposed to be soothing.

The Green Room

This part of the house includes the lobby, box office, and marquee, the portion of a performance venue that is open to the public beyond the audience hall.

Front of the house

The farthest reaches of the audience seating area away from the stage are called this.

Back of the house

When a show is over and everyone leaves the theater, the last person out, perhaps the stage manager, places this light downstage center to ward off any bad luck spirits. In an Equity theater, it signifies that you're off the clock; anyone still in the theater knows they are no longer on the job.

Ghost light or Equity light

Bonus question: What famous poet, playwright, and actor began a monologue with the phrase that titles this section?

William Shakespeare

6. THE SILVER SCREEN

A Broadway performer and specialty dancer in Hollywood musicals, this jazz and ballet dancer is known for his role as one of the brothers in the 1954 film *Seven Brides for Seven Brothers*.

Matt Mattox

This choreographer was less concerned with dancers' technique than with their ability to form geometric patterns and shapes with their bodies, so that he could use over-the-top camera angles to create a bird's-eye, kaleidoscope view of his choreography.

Busby Berkeley

This producer, director, and choreographer is known for directing the films *Hocus Pocus*, the *High School Musical* series, *The Rocky Horror Picture Show*, *Cheetah Girls 2*, and *Michael Jackson's This Is It* concert and film. His choreography works include *Ferris Bueller's Day Off*, *Pretty in Pink*, and *Dirty Dancing*.

Kenny Ortega

This dancer, actor, singer, director, and choreographer went to college for journalism, dropped out, worked to help his family financially, went back to college, and then entered law school. He had success in such films as *For Me and My Gal*, *Anchors Aweigh*, *On the Town*, and in what was voted the single most popular musical movie of all time, *Singin' in the Rain*.

Gene Kelly

She started as a ballerina and acrobat and was hailed as the World's Greatest Female Tapper by Dance Masters of America. In 1929, she made her Broadway debut in *Follow Thru*. She danced with Fred Astaire in big movie musicals and worked alongside top actors such as George Murphy and James Stewart.

Eleanor Powell

This Academy Award-winning actress, singer, and dancer appeared in more than seventy films, including *Stage Door* and *Kitty Foyle*. She became the highest-paid woman in America and is known for her cinematic partnership with Fred Astaire. The famous line from a 1982 Frank & Ernest cartoon, "Sure he was great, but don't forget that she did everything he did... backwards and in high heels" was inspired by their partnership.

Ginger Rogers

This triple-threat performer started his career in vaudeville with his older sister, who was actually the more successful dancer at the time. He danced professionally until he was seventy and, of the ten movie musicals he made between 1933 and 1939, he partnered with Ginger Rogers in all but one.

Fred Astaire

In 2001, this choreographer, director, and producer opened a dance studio in LA named DADA, an acronym. She was in the original cast of *Fame* and her monologue went like this: "You want to become a dancer? You're going to have to work. You've got big dreams? You want fame? Well, fame costs. And right here's where you start paying in sweat."

Debbie Allen

This Russian dancer rose to international stardom in the 1970s and his success as an actor earned him Academy Award and Golden Globe nominations. He played one of Carrie Bradshaw's love interests in *Sex in the City*, and two of his films are *The Turning Point* and *White Nights*.

Mikhail Baryshnikov

This Tony Award-winning triple threat studied under Henry LeTang, and began his career performing in nightclubs with his father, Maurice, Sr., and brother, Maurice, Jr. Film credits include *Tap*, *The Cotton Club*, and playing opposite Mikhail Baryshnikov in *White Nights*.

Gregory Hines

A movie producer "discovered" her while she was an understudy in *The Pajama Game*. This Golden Globe and Academy Award winner has authored many books, and in 2013 received a Kennedy Center Honor for her lifetime contribution to American culture. Her film debut was in Alfred Hitchcock's *The Trouble with Harry*.

Shirley MacLaine

7. NAMES TO KNOW

Since her 1963 college graduation, she has written books, started her own dance company, received one Tony, two Emmys, and nineteen honorary doctorates for her work, which includes over 129 dances, twelve television specials, six Hollywood movies, four full-length ballets, and four Broadway shows.

Twyla Tharp

In 1998, according to Guinness World Records, this dancer achieved the record for fastest taps per second—thirty-five taps—and in the year 2000, he was the highest-paid dancer worldwide, earning $1,600,000 per week.

Michael Flatley

He is the founder of the award-winning group The Groovaloos, the first hip hop company to tour and play Off Broadway with a stage show based on true stories of their own lives. You may have seen him dancing on the freeway in the opening scene of *La La Land*.

Bradley "Shooz" Rapier

Known for her roles in *The Firebird* and *The Nutcracker*, this dancer is considered America's first Native American prima ballerina. She received a Kennedy Center Honor for her lifetime achievements in the performing arts, was inducted into the National Women's Hall of Fame, and was once married to George Balanchine.

Maria Tallchief

This native Texas tapper choreographed and acted in *My One and Only*. His accolades include ten Tony Awards, three Astaire Awards, and a National Medal of Arts from the President of the United States. His film credits include *Hello Dolly* and *The Boy Friend*. He celebrated his golden decade by touring with his one-man show *Taps, Tunes, and Tall Tales*.

Tommy Tune

Dancers wear one-piece garments, originally called *maillot*, that cover the torso and leave the legs free. This famous French acrobat and circus performer created that garment to show off his physique. He was also the subject of the 19th-century song "Daring Young Man on the Flying Trapeze."

Jules Leotard

He created a company in his name that has performed for an estimated 25 million people in seventy-one countries across six continents since 1958. His best known and most viewed modern dance performance work is *Revelations*.

Alvin Ailey

Antonia Basilotta, later and better known by this name, helped found The Lockers, a group that forever changed street dance in America. She created the one-hit wonder *Mickey*. Yes, the cheerleader song and video.

Toni Basil

This famous B-Boy was a member of Rock Steady Crew, The Electric Boogaloos, Tribal Click, and Zulu Nation. He is one of the most dynamic and influential figures in hip hop culture, renowned for his graffiti art and his incredible knowledge of hip hop history, as well as his popping, tutting, and breaking skills.

Mr. Wiggles

This two-time Tony Award-winning choreographer ran track in college and discovered dance at age 19. His choreography is known for challenging philosophical and social issues relating to race, identity, and terminal illness. He received the Kennedy Center Honors in 2010. You may know him best as the choreographer of Broadway's *Spring Awakening*.

Bill T. Jones

All That Jazz, a semiautobiographical film about a dying workaholic, received four Academy Awards and was nominated for five others. This choreographer and director, who became known for his intricate jazz style favoring pigeon toes, is the record holder for the most Tony awards, with eight for choreography and one for direction.

Bob Fosse

Well known for her Broadway success in *Can Can*, *Damn Yankees*, and *Chicago*, this triple threat began as a young child who wore corrective boots to straighten her legs from rickets. She became a four-time Tony Award winner and was a spouse to Bob Fosse.

Gwen Verdon

Her choreography is infused with social, political, and psychological ideas made timeless by their deep connection with the audience. She was the first dancer to perform at the White House, and her style grew from her experimentation with the opposing movements of contraction and release.

Martha Graham

Born a twin and the son of a dance teacher who founded her studio in the basement of their home, this pioneer has been a student, competition dancer, professional dancer, choreographer, teacher, educational columnist, and owner and publisher of *Dance Life* magazine.

Rhee Gold

This past principal with Alvin Ailey American Dance Theater and the American Ballet Theater appeared on Broadway in the premiere cast of *Fosse*. He is co-founder and co-artistic director of Complexions Contemporary Ballet.

Desmond Richardson

Known as "the man who danced with Fred Astaire," this dance director and choreographer is an Academy Award and Emmy winner who choreographed over fifty films. The classics he did with Fred Astaire and Ginger Rogers were career highlights.

Hermes Pan

Having survived polio as a child, she was encouraged by her father to take ballet to help strengthen her frail body. By age 13, she was dancing with the Ballet Russe de Monte Carlo. You may know her from her celebrated partnering scenes with Fred Astaire and Gene Kelly or her leading role in *The Band Wagon*.

Cyd Charisse

A skinny tapper from Pennsylvania boarded a bus to New York with $130 and a dream to dance on Broadway. He was cast in the original company of *West Side Story*. His website, Answers4Dancers.com, was founded with the mission of empowering dancers and choreographers to create successful careers for themselves.

Grover Dale

8. LINGO LANGUAGE

Individuals who are offered a job, bypassing the audition process because of their excellent reputations, are said to do this.

Direct book

This chief position, often held by the dance captain of a show, requires a performer to learn and understudy both a wide range of parts in the chorus and lead roles, all at the same time.

Swing

The "B" in the hip hop term "B-boy" stands for this.

Break Boy or Bronx Boy

An audition that is open to everyone, even those not part of a theatrical union, goes by this name. Cows can't point their toes, nor do they audition, but if they did, you'd certainly see them there.

Cattle call

Performers use this word prior to a performance to wish one another good luck. The word dates back to the days when Parisian streets were so filled with what's left by horse-drawn carriages that actors regularly had to avoid stepping in dung before going into the theater.

"Merde" (pronounced "maird")

Wishing someone good luck before a performance is considered bad luck. Instead, dancers and other performers tell each other this as the standard way of saying, "Have a great show."

"Break a leg"

Many Broadway theatres showing musicals are said to be this on Monday nights because they have Sunday matinees.

Dark

Ballet choreography for two people is this.

Pas de deux

The art of developing routines by linking together several moves or techniques, often set to music, is called this.

Choreography

When dancers express themselves by extemporizing or flowing off the vibes of the music, they are doing this.

Freestyle

A freestyle session in which dancers "battle" each other, usually in a circle, by taking turns at improvising movement and creatively expressing how they perceive the music.

Jam

She was the goddess of dance and one of the nine Greek muses; she musically accompanied dancers with her lyre.

Terpsichore (pronounced "turp-SIK-uh-ree")

Some performers proudly refer to themselves as this, meaning a free spirited person who follows an unconventional career path of seasonal work, continually reinventing him- or herself. It is also the name of a 1959 Broadway musical.

Gypsy

9. JAZZ GYPSIES

This dancer began his career in ballet and modern and went on to choreograph for the camera, integrating styles from India, Africa, and South America with the Lindy Hop and Cecchetti ballet technique. It's no wonder he earned the title "The Father of (Theatrical) Jazz Dance."

Jack Cole

Her career started at age 13 when she performed as a singer and dancer with the Los Angeles Civic Light Opera. She transitioned from stage to screen, and the highlight of her success was her Golden Globe Award-winning performance in the movie South Pacific. Other notable films include *There's No Business Like Show Business and Anything Goes.*

Mitzi Gaynor

A modern dancer known for his socially conscious works expressing racial issues, he earned an Emmy nomination and a Tony win. He has choreographed worldwide for over ninety dance companies and was referred to as one of America's most irreplaceable dance treasures.

Donald McKayle

His career began to thrive when Universal Studios cast him as one of fourteen in a tap dancing group called Jivin' Jacks and Jills. In 1953 he was best known as an action model for Walt Disney's Peter Pan. His act, The Dupree Trio, contributed to what is now referred to as "West Coast Jazz."

Roland Dupree

Born Milton Greenwald, he was studying chemical engineering at college when he fell in love with modern dance and left school. He received a scholarship to the School of American Ballet and in 1942 adopted the name under which he won five Tony Awards. Some of his most famous works include Tony Award-winning *Finian's Rainbow* and *Guys and Dolls* on Broadway, and Hollywood film adaptions of musicals such as *Band Wagon* and *Seven Brides for Seven Brothers*.

Michael Kidd

This jazz dancer, master teacher, choreographer, and author of *Anthology of American Jazz Dance* has performed on Broadway and in theater and film, and is the founder of one of Chicago's top professional dance companies and the five-day celebration, Jazz Dance World Congress.

Gus Giordano

This Emmy Award-winning Brooklyn native has credits as a producer, director, and choreographer. From Tony, Grammy, and Academy Award shows to specials for Barry Manilow, Dean Martin, Bing Crosby, Bob Hope, and Jerry Lewis, and work in films such as *Pee Wee's Playhouse Adventure* and *Solid Gold*, this man has seemingly done it all.

Kevin Carlisle

After a serious car accident left him paralyzed, this jazz dancer created a series of exercises, expressive movements, and oppositional rib stretches to help rehabilitate his body. His real name is Eugene Facciuto, but you probably know him by this nickname, which was given to him by his friend and fellow dancer Gene Kelly.

Luigi

This three-time Emmy winner restaged the works of Jerome Robbins and brought a *West Side Story* style of dance to Gap commercials in 2000. He choreographed dance scenes for many of Mel Brooks' films, including "Puttin' on the Ritz" in *Young Frankenstein*.

Alan Johnson

This three-time Tony Award winner is an actor, singer, and dancer trained under George Balanchine. One of his most memorable roles was on Broadway as the Scarecrow in *The Wiz*. He was the first to portray that role.

Hinton Battle

This Swedish-born actress, singer, dancer, and winner of an Emmy and five Golden Globes also received nominations for two Academy Awards, two Grammy Awards, a Screen Actors Guild Award, and six Emmy Awards. You may have seen her in movies like *Bye Bye Birdie*, *Viva Las Vegas*, *Grumpy Old Men*, and *Grumpier Old Men*.

Ann-Margret

This Tony Award-winning director, writer, and choreographer dropped out of high school and toured with *West Side Story* in the role of Baby John. His most successful shows on Broadway are *A Chorus Line* and *Dreamgirls*.

Michael Bennett

She is noted for founding a highly respected professional dance ensemble. She owns a studio in Denver and holds to a philosophy of "One Spirit, Many Voices," which is reflected in all that she does.

Cleo Parker Robinson

This original member of the Alvin Ailey Dance Company has film credits that include *The Color Purple*, *Roots*, and *King Kong*.

Claude Thompson

He was a first-level dancer with Julliard Dance and went on to create a memorable performance as Loco in the film *West Side Story*. He created works for over forty different television series such as *Fame*, and thirty different television specials, including *The Sonny and Cher Show*.

Jaime Rogers

Known as "The Doctor of Jazz," he taught many styles of dance, including his own signature jazz named "VOP" for the sound he made to get energy out of his dancers. In 1982, this Emmy Award-winning choreographer helped establish the Broadway Dance Center.

Frank Hatchett

10. ANYTHING GOES

A British musical hit telling the story of a boy who loves to dance and struggles with the negative stereotypes associated with male dancers was made into a movie, and began this trend, in which more boys confidently pursue and succeed as professional dancers.

The Billy Elliott effect

Bees communicate by touch, smell, and this.

Dance

In the song "Mr. Bojangles," the lyrics express grief about the loss of this kind of pet.

A dog

International Dance Day is the 29th of this month.

April

National Dance Day was acknowledged by the United States Congress in 2010. On this day in 2012, the U.S. Postal Service paid tribute to these four influential choreographers by giving them their own stamps.

Isadora Duncan, José Limón, Katherine Dunham, and Bob Fosse

Myths, folklore, and performance rituals abound in the theater. One superstition forbids performers to exit the dressing room left foot first, and another to take this before you believe you deserve it.

A bow"

This shoe company, named for its founder, a dancer, is well known for professional dance shoes handmade from Italian leather; they can be seen on some of today's biggest dance stars.

LaDuca Shoes

A common theater superstition is that a perfect dress rehearsal signals a very short performance run. The saying goes that a bad dress rehearsal will result in this.

A great opening show

This First Lady of the United States performed with the Martha Graham Company and went on to establish an addiction clinic in her name.

Choreography

11. TAP-ABLE TAP-TATIONS

May 25th is National Tap Dance Day in the United States. It marks the birthday of this famous tap dancer, who danced on the silver screen with Shirley Temple in the 1930s, making history as the first interracial couple to dance on film.

Bill 'Bojangles' Robinson

This jazz and tap dancer has won countless awards, including an Emmy for The Tap Dance Kid.

Phil Black

Some called him "the Ace of Taps." His dance troupe were regulars on The Perry Como Show and, according to the Library of Congress, he holds the distinction of being the choreographer who has appeared in the most films performing his own work.

Louis DaPron

Mikhail Baryshnikow named this team of dancing siblings "perfect examples of pure genius." Fred Astaire said of their tap dancing finale in the film Stormy Weather, which featured the brothers, "This dance number is the greatest movie musical sequence I have ever seen."

The Nicholas Brothers

Every August, thousands of tap dancers gather at Herald Square for this event, sponsored by Macy's, which holds several Guinness World Records for the largest assembly of tap dancers performing a single routine at the same time and place.

Tap-o-Mania

Born Johnnie Lucille Collier, she adopted this stage name and had a successful career famed for her speedy tap skills and roles in films like Easter Parade, On the Town, and Kiss Me Kate.

Ann Miller

If you recognize the names of these great performers, you love this art form: Jimmy Slyde, Chuck Green, Howard "Sandman" Sims, Steve Condos, Lon Chaney, Harold "Stumpy" Cromer, Dianne Walker, Charles "Honi" Coles, Bill Bailey, Charles "Cholly" Atkins, Eddie Brown, Arthur Duncan, Jeni LeGon, Clayton "Peg Leg" Bates, Bunny Briggs, Charles "Cookie" Cook, Frances Nealy, Earnest "Brownie" Brown, King Rastas Brown, and Harriet "Quicksand" Browne.

Tap

12.   ICONIC VIDEOS

MC Hammer made harem pants a popular article of clothing when he wore them to dance in this music video of his.

"U Can't Touch This"

This is the most popular music video of all time.

"Thriller"

Britney Spears was an aspiring dancer who competed in dance competitions before she dominated 1990s pop music with this famous single.

"Hit Me Baby One More Time"

In 1998, Paula Abdul choreographed the black and white video for this single, winning MTV Music Awards for best female video, best choreography, and best dance video.

"Straight Up"

Janet Jackson took a political stand in 1989 and topped worldwide charts with this socially conscious song and video.

"Rhythm Nation"

In 1986, this expensive short-form music video production choreographed by Michael Peters and sung by Lionel Richie had everyone's world flipped upside down.

"Dancing on the Ceiling"

Nominated for Best Group Video in the 1987 MTV Video Music Awards, this video had ordinary people, famous figures, and famous objects all dancing in the same pose. Not only was it a catchy tune sung by The Bangles, it broke barriers by being the first song sung by an all-female group who also played most of the instruments.

"Walk Like an Egyptian"

Madonna began her career on a dance university scholarship, was awarded a six-week course of study with Alvin Ailey American Dance Theater, and then decided to move to New York to pursue a dance career. She transitioned to music and became known for inspiring dancers to "strike a pose" in this music video.

"Vogue"

SECTION 6
DANCE INTO LIFE

26. YOU HAVE A VOICE... USE IT

Speak your mind—even if your voice shakes.
~ Maggie Kuhn

Standing up for yourself and being assertive is not about being rude, pushy, mean, or aggressive. It's about finding a way for you to be comfortable when asking for what you want in a way that respects others and that others respect.

If you find yourself unhappy with how you're being treated... if you feel that you're always being taken for granted or used by some of the people in your life, then do a self-check, look for patterns, or find ways to set boundaries.

If you have difficulty communicating what is or is not acceptable to you, research this subject to learn more about the ways in which we teach people what we will and will not tolerate from them.

Treating yourself well is what sets the standard for others to follow. If you don't feel good about yourself, you lose power because you think you don't have any. Consider your power. It's there.

Stomping into the Savoy. When I was 13 years old, I was part of a boys' youth group. Our headmaster, our leader, was a local farmer. He was this slumped-over guy who needed to take a ballet class to learn how to stand up straight. His outlook on life was as bleak as his posture. He had no smile, no charisma, no nothing. As far as I was concerned, he was ill-equipped to lead, even though he was a decent and kind person.

One day he said to all of us, "Boys, life is hard, and it's gunna git harder with the years. Yep. Life is a tough row to hoe. So y'all best git ready now."

To this day, I don't know what came over me, but out of nowhere I stood up and shouted, "That's not true. And I don't believe it for one second." Since I was an extremely shy kid, I stunned myself doing this. Up to that point in my life, I'd never really taken a stand on much of anything.

Years later, while working on location in Garrison, New York, on the movie *Hello, Dolly!* I did something else rather bold. I asked the choreographer, Michael Kidd, if I could speak with him and the film's director, Gene Kelly. After Michael called Gene over, I proceeded to explain that I wanted off the film because I was in so few scenes and had other jobs awaiting me back home in Los Angeles. Bottom line was that the assistant choreographer on the film didn't like me—imagine that!—and she was making the selections for all the scenes.

I couldn't believe I was telling two major stars I didn't want to work with them anymore. Yet they understood. What's more, it turned out they did value my contribution. They overrode the assistant choreographer's bias. From that point on, I was in more scenes, and I stayed on the film until the end.

Another time, I was touring the country with my dear friend, the late Debbie Reynolds. She had a big show with lots of singers and dancers, and I was both lead dancer and dance captain. I ran the rehearsals while we were on the road. Debbie told me she would be late for our next rehearsal, but we agreed on how I would proceed until she got there. The full orchestra, the entire cast, and all the stagehands were present. I was standing downstage center when the stage manager informed me that, due to a logistical issue, we couldn't begin where Debbie had instructed me to begin. So I made the decision to rehearse another section because, well, time is money.

We were 30 minutes into rehearsal when I saw Debbie approach me from the back of the house, getting hotter and hotter with each step. When she reached me, she shouted, "What are you doing?" Before I could explain why we hadn't been able to rehearse the section she'd asked me to, she snapped her fingers and shouted, "No, no, no. That's not what we discussed." She started yelling at me in front of everyone.

Now, mind you, I had a live microphone in my hand. I let it go, and it crashed to the floor with ear-piercing feedback. I walked to my dance bag, snapped it up, and began my exit. I walked through all the performers and orchestra musicians and out the back of the theater. I saw Debbie's limo with her driver in it. I knew him. I hopped in and said, "Take me to the hotel." I was mad.

A few hours later, just as I was about to shower, the phone rang. A little voice squealed, "Hi, Joey. It's Deb. What're you doing?"

"I'm about to drown my sorrows," I replied. "What do you want?"

"I'm really sorry about today. I misunderstood," she said, her voice still little.

"Fine," I said. "That's good. Now don't ever do that again." I hung up the phone. We remained best friends from then on.

On another occasion, while staging Diana Ross's world tour in the early 1970s, I was in London, staying at the Savoy Hotel. I'd already been up for two days and nights preparing for the show's opening. I was tired.

As Diana and I discussed what she wanted for a particular section, her voice escalated, and within seconds she was screaming at me. I must have a thing for dropping whatever I'm holding because I let go of two handfuls of loose papers. I was out the door before they hit the floor, and I left Ms. Ross standing there by her lonesome. I was so upset that when I arrived at the hotel, I literally stomped into the Savoy.

Diana apologized the following morning, and for the rest of our time together she refused to go anywhere without me. She had this mink coat that went with us everywhere. She'd ask me to carry it and I would. What an entrance we made.

The moral of these stories? Stand up for yourself. The people you're working with need to understand that you're there for the same reason they are: to do what's best for the show, project, or whatever it is you're working on. Trust yourself enough to walk away when something doesn't feel right. In other words, look out for yourself. You are *not* a doormat, so don't act like one. ✦

THE PEOPLE YOU'RE WORKING WITH NEED TO UNDERSTAND THAT YOU'RE THERE FOR THE SAME REASON THEY ARE: TO DO WHAT'S BEST FOR THE SHOW, PROJECT, OR WHATEVER IT IS YOU'RE WORKING ON.

THE BEST,
MOST
SIGNIFICANT
RELATIONSHIP
YOU'LL EVER
HAVE IS THE
ONE WITH
YOURSELF.

Silence Speaks Volumes. Joe drops what he's holding in his hands, I drop golden silence. I've learned to let people say what they need to say while noting what's not worth a reply. If someone says something crazy to me, I gaze at them while thinking, *Wow, too bad ignorance doesn't hurt.* If I respond at all, I take my voice up an octave and say, "Oh. O.K."—leaving a few seconds between those two words for heightened effect. When my buttons get pushed, I talk myself into letting go of the fire within because I'm trying to mitigate the drama. I stand up for myself by arguing with no one. I save my energy for more important undertakings like writing a book while sitting on airplanes.

I've sat next to people on flights who, after finding out I'm a tap dancer, will say something like, "So you travel around teaching tap, eh? Oh, that's nice, but, umm, you sound intelligent." I don't know if that's a statement about tap dancers or black people.

On one flight, a man watched me work on my laptop for three hours. When we touched down, he finally asked what I was doing. Perhaps I exceeded his low expectations because when I told him I was writing a book, he asked, in the snarliest, nastiest tone imaginable, "Well, who *are* you?" I calmly replied, "Sir, I put on my pants the same way you do: one leg at a time."

Robert Frost wrote this: "Education is the ability to listen to almost anything without losing your temper or your self-confidence." I grew up in a big family, and I learned how to choose battles with care. You can't fight every situation or argue every point. Hum a show tune to yourself and recognize when it's O.K. to keep your truths to yourself. Sharing opinions, needing to be right, or having the last word are overrated, and there's simply not enough time in life for back-and-forth contending. Find your way to stay calm during those moments when you know that your next response is everything. Silence, even just a few seconds, gives you time … to think about what to do or say any time of the day. ✦

27. YOUR ART COMES TO LIFE THROUGH YOU

The only thing worse than starting something and failing is not starting something.

~ Seth Godin

There's only so much you can learn from a book, mentor, seminar, podcast, or video. There's only so much other people can do in support of you, your talent, and your ambitions. There comes a time when you unequivocally must decide that today is the day, the time is now, and *you* are the one to start your art.

To Win, You Have To Earn It. Sorry to break it to you, but there's no such thing as overnight success. There may be some overnight sensations, but they're rare. The reason you're bombarded with news about the few who meet with incredible luck is because they *are* so rare. I wouldn't call it success, what those few have met with.

Research the backstory of any high achiever and you're likely to find decades of sweat, tears, and work.

In my experiences on the stage, screen, and convention circuit, working with my fair share of celebrities, the one trait I've noticed in all high achievers is tunnel vision. They know exactly and precisely what they want, and they put their energy into pursuing it. Sure, passion is necessary and it's great, but it takes more than that. Besides, we have many passions during our lifetimes, and they can change as we pass through different stages.

If "fame and fortune" is your goal, then what are you going to do for it? You gotta put in the work. And if you don't, then don't be upset by the results you didn't get from the work you didn't do. Nobody is going to hand you your dream, and there are no shortcuts, *mon chère.* If you do happen to hear about a shortcut, put up your antennae. Because if something doesn't sound right, or things don't add up, you need to be able to put two and two together.

Bella Malinka, a teacher at the High School of Performing Arts in New York City, said, "You never conquer ballet, you make peace with it!" Some aspects of life are like that. We all go through rough patches, and we all hit a few bumps along the way. But we manage. We make it through and we get back out there and try again.

Hard work doesn't necessarily guarantee that every now and then things won't go crazy. But when you're prepared, you can go with the flow. You get yourself together and try again. "I have not failed. I've just found 10,000 ways that won't work," said Thomas Edison. I love that quote. Stay curious and keep looking for solutions.

WHAT MATTERS MORE THAN WHERE YOU ARE RIGHT NOW IS WHAT YOU DO NEXT.

SORRY TO BREAK IT TO YOU, BUT THERE'S NO SUCH THING AS OVERNIGHT SUCCESS. THERE MAY BE SOME OVERNIGHT SENSATIONS, BUT THEY'RE RARE.

I used to say that many are called, but few are chosen. Today, however, because of technology, things have changed. Now you have the tools to pretty much do anything. You can learn what you want, where and when you want to. Learning tools and resources are at your disposal. You can make yourself a standout, if that's what you want. Are you old enough to know who Coco Chanel is? She said, "In order to be irreplaceable, one must always be different."

Your mindset is first and foremost. Once that's in positive working order, you can go for what you want. You have what it takes, just like anyone else. It all comes down to how badly you want it... or, in some cases like yours truly, how badly you need it. ◆

"NOW TRENDING" COULD BE SOMETHING *YOU* START.

There's only so much time you can spend adjusting who you are to fit in, or pretending to be like others, before you lose yourself in the opinions and styles of your peers. Those who are threatened by disruptions to the status quo, busy chasing the next big thing, or unable to adapt to change make themselves easy to overlook. Those who sit back, not wanting to draw attention their way, just wait for the next big thing to come along. Invariably it does, and they latch on to it as if experiencing a kind of unconscious paralysis. You may notice that they appear at times slightly uncomfortable, a tad awkward, and even a bit silly in their trend-following. The mob is not necessarily doing the important work.

You're not here to keep things the same, hide your voice, lay low, or hang back in the mediocrity that forms the collective average. Treat your talents with respect and do what *you* were made to do. Some of us will be remembered for the "rules" we break, and for interrupting business as usual.

"Someday" Isn't a Day of the Week. What you *plan* to do and what you do are two different things. While an idea written down on a piece of paper is a great start, it isn't the biggest or most important part of the equation. Technology has transformed us into efficient information gatherers, but ideas are of little value if they're not acted upon. Practice your artistry today because action is as important as information. Get off your derrière and bring your art to life. Share. Love. Repeat.

It's About To Be A Thing. Whether everything old is new again, or what's new is a compilation of the old, it's just a matter of time before what's next is right now. History will be made. Because when the love of a subject serves as the foundation for your life and career—both in service to yourself and others—expect a *chef-d'oeuvre*. A masterpiece.

YOU DON'T HAVE TO BE AMAZING TO START, BUT YOU HAVE TO
START TO GET TO AMAZING.

28. TREAT YOURSELF TO LIFE

Live a good honorable life. Then when you get older and think back,
you'll be able to enjoy it a second time.

~ *Dalai Lama*

That something inside of you begging to be unleashed, urging you day after day to go for it, that's your calling. The *moving* art you want to launch, market, book, produce, record, host, or perform wants you. The best way to know if something is for you is to give it a go. Say yes to your innately distinctive voice. As you do, you'll understand more and more about the contribution you will make—and understand it better and more quickly than you ever could from reading mags, watching vids, and observing from the sidelines.

Whether you flea hop or grand jeté, get as close to the real thing as possible. Move toward where the sun shines and the rain falls on what you love. Breathe it, live it, and then decide how to build your world around it. Because you, your ideals, and what you have to say matter. Truth.

A Sweet Life Isn't the Cause of Happiness—It's the Result of It. I love Toastmasters International, and I became a member while in graduate school. It's a communication and leadership development organization. Basically, you give speeches and you get feedback. I joined because too few people could understand, either audibly or logically, anything I was saying. I've had my share of academic challenges.

Table Topics is one of the organization's many traditions. In it, respondents are called on at random to speak impromptu on a topic or question. At my very first meeting I was asked to speak on happiness. I used my two minutes to object to the notion that happiness existed. I came right out and said it: "There's no such thing as happiness." I complained and griped about how even the sound of the word made my skin crawl, and how mad I got when anyone used it. I concluded my talk by announcing to my audience—people I hadn't met until that evening—that standing before them and having to use the word had just about ruined my day and my mood. I was seriously cynical.

As a kid, the only place I'd seen happiness was on television sitcoms and talk shows. Years later, while watching two of Oprah's shows, on both occasions I was struck by a guest spending her entire time discussing how happy she was in her life. I assumed that both Tina Turner and Barbra Streisand were lying.

Around the same time, one of my older sisters admonished me for my all-day, everyday sarcastic and pessimistic view of everything. She said I was incredibly annoying.

At first I couldn't see it. But, over time, I began to pay attention to what my mind was doing, and finally I realized that my sister was right. I didn't have one good thought on any subject. Probably all of us question our paths, or an aspect of our lives, some of the time. But. No one should live in a doubting state 24/7.

Once I achieved this awareness, I set out to use my life as a test to see if Tina and Barbra were telling the truth. In other words, my motivation for everything, including my decision to leave my desk job and tap dance for a living, became the search for happiness.

My first objective? *Change the way my mind works.* It took years to switch my thoughts from looking at everything wrong to seeing what was actually right. Sounds so simple, doesn't it?

My second objective? *Stop complaining.* That was easy. I just shut up and kept my thoughts to myself—which also helped eliminate arguing with anyone about anything.

My third objective? *Take responsibility for every aspect of my life.* Since we all have different experiences, this will mean something different for each person. Investigate this concept to determine what it means for you and then apply the idea to your own life and be honest—because, well, that's the point.

Taking responsibility for my life led me directly to the concept of forgiveness, including self-forgiveness. Either way, showing yourself love and grace is a *thing,* and forgiveness is ultimately something you do for yourself. Since the years pass quickly, may I suggest that you keep the idea of forgiveness "top of mind"? That is, hold onto it as a real possibility and option.

For situations in which you're not quite ready to channel your inner Elsa and let it go, stay open to the idea of forgiveness. The *willingness* to forgive, in itself, will create some peace of mind—and that's worth pursuing.

My final objective? *Get some help.* Again, we each experience and respond to life differently. Split-second decisions can change your world, so ask yourself if you're willing to endure the consequences, should it ever come to that. Think each decision through and find out if what you want is worth the risk. Remember also that "slow and steady" works. Choose healthy, mature, and responsible ways to cope with life. Help by way of therapy, mentorship, sponsorship, and friendships are options. You are never alone.

Today, I understand that happiness exists right there where you're standing. I spent years trying to comprehend how that was possible. Here's what I came up with: The search so many pursue outside themselves is actually a search we must pursue within ourselves.

Happiness, contentment, and fulfillment are yours. You don't need to wait for something outside of yourself, nor do you need a particular condition or circumstance to create it, even when you're surrounded by those who think otherwise. Your happy dreams live *in* you. You're the miracle. Stop looking.

Your qualities aren't static. You can, at will, change your thoughts to call upon your version of calm, cool, and composed. You can discover simple ways to make moments and days special and to foster positive vibes in a negative situation. Yes. This stuff takes practice, which if you're a dancer, you know very well how to do. With practice, deliberate and conscious shifts in perception will happen, offering a peace that passes human understanding. ✦

FUNDAMENTAL HAPPINESS PRINCIPLE: THE GOOD THINGS YOU WANT FOR YOURSELF? WANT THOSE SAME THINGS FOR OTHERS.

WITH PRACTICE, DELIBERATE AND CONSCIOUS SHIFTS IN PERCEPTION WILL HAPPEN, OFFERING A PEACE THAT PASSES HUMAN UNDERSTANDING.

ADVERSITY CAN MAKE YOU STRONGER—THAT, PLUS LIFTING WEIGHTS.

Some people have tons of advantages and do nothing with their gifts, while others, against seemingly impossible odds, use what they have and build a meaningful, high-performance, and enjoyable life. Some celebrities may be household names today, but their journeys haven't been without a share of hardship. Before achieving success, a few of them lived in their cars. Others had to drop out of school to support their families. Still others held modest first jobs as street mime performers, oyster shuckers, restaurant belly dancers, ice cream scoopers, hair salon sweepers, and chicken restaurant mascots.

Yet not everyone has a humble beginning story or has to struggle to make ends meet. Adversity isn't what's important. Many of the world's happiest and most accomplished individuals, non-celebrity types included, who have achieved even a modicum of success credit their accomplishments to days, weeks, and years of diligent effort because, as you know, anything worthwhile takes time to build.

Progress, Not Perfection. Persist and you'll prevail, right? Yes. But persistence is of little value if the place you've started from, the place you're accustomed to being in, isn't where you really belong. Or, maybe you're not sure where you're going, unclear about the expected result, or facing the wrong way. Sometimes you'll listen to that small inner voice, heed your own sage counsel, and still make a mistake or misstep. Stuff happens, and it's unrealistic to expect guarantees at every juncture.

Forgive yourself for the half-completed projects and for the ventures you quit after a few attempts. Inactivity during any days, weeks, or years needn't justify the same behavior moving forward. The solution for occasional falls or stalls is to plant again. Plant more seeds in advance of the harvest you expect tomorrow. Lack of motivation in one area doesn't tell your whole story.

Talk to Yourself Instead of Listening to Yourself. No one is more aware of your minor imperfections than you are. Instead of finding fault, listing flaws, berating yourself, and being your own worst critic—this will sound corny—be your best friend. Make statements of certainty about yourself and reference what you want, not what you don't want.

SHIFT HAPPENS.

There's a lot in life you can't control—and, equally, there's a lot you can. Life alters and finds its way despite any efforts on your part to keep things as you like them. When change beckons, and brings along its friend discomfort, accept what you're powerless over and cope in healthy and responsible ways. You can't control every situation. Make peace with occasional imperfection, and respect experience for the teacher it is. Nothing is ever a complete failure if you've learned from it.

LIVE. CHOOSE. LEARN. CHOOSE BETTER.

You're going to do more than one thing with your life. You'll travel different roads, and not all of them will be picture-perfect or smooth. It may take a while to figure out what you want, and then more time to find your way, so forget about setting time limits or a particular threshold for achieving success. Sometimes you may have to slow down to speed up. Just because you've traveled some distance on a particular road doesn't mean you have to keep going down it. You can make a different decision because life, like the hokey pokey, allows for U-turns.

TALK NICE TO YOURSELF, LIKE THE WAY YOU WOULD TO SOMEONE YOU LOVE.

Find Your Rhythm, Find Your Life. What skills do you need to develop your craft? And I'm not just talking about your dancing. I'm talking about your very own unique Womp Bop A Looma A Womp Bam Boom. What skills do you bring to the table unrelated to dance that can help build your career and life *around* dance?

For me, it's my organization skills. I apparently took my cues from Charles Dickens, who said, "I never could have done what I have done without the habits of punctuality, order, and diligence, without the determination to concentrate myself on one subject at a time." There you have it.

I worked hard to develop the habits I needed to continue to grow as a businessperson. You have to develop your business skills, because without them where will you be? Backstage somewhere crying, I guess.

You have an aptitude for something exceptional, and I can't tell you what that is. I *can* tell you, however, that your dance training, regardless of whether it's primary or secondary in your life, can lead you toward discovering more about yourself and your talents. Pay attention to what gets you excited, and work to develop your skills around that. You owe it to yourself to make your unique contribution to the world.

Whatever your dream—and I don't care how old you are; what you look like; what your skin color, number of chromosomes, or financial status is; what your parents do or did for a living; what church you attend; or whom you love—you are *not* a failure just because you haven't achieved notoriety by the age of 31, 41, 51, or 61. That's the most ridiculous thing I've ever heard, and anyone who thinks that way is never going to make it. Julie Adler, my business partner, turned 60 the year we started Tremaine Dance Conventions.

Even if you don't yet know what you want, keep your mind positive. Never tell yourself you're too washed up or not good enough. Thinking *I'm too old*, *I'm too broke*, or *I'm too far down the road* will not get you anywhere.

And, if your motivation wanes, go take a dance class. That'll do it. (Well, for that matter, you can take a dance class anytime. It's only going to make things that much better.)

You can't control every aspect of your life. But, thank goodness, you can control your thoughts, which just happen to control your actions. A positive mindset will help your rhythm more than a negative one will. Treat yourself to a good life. Oh—and one more thing. We're on this earth to help each other. And if you can't help, please don't hurt each other. Thank you very much. Over, done, and finished. ◆

HAVE YOUR CAKE.

YOU CAN'T CONTROL EVERY ASPECT OF YOUR LIFE. BUT, THANK GOODNESS, YOU CAN CONTROL YOUR THOUGHTS, WHICH JUST HAPPEN TO CONTROL YOUR ACTIONS.

29. AND ANOTHER THING...

Please go for your dreams.
Whatever your ideals, you can become whatever you want to become.

~ Michael Jackson

What you want is your thing—something only you can do... and, yes, you can do it and perhaps allow dance as your springboard to creating a life and career you're proud of.

We conclude our book with two powerful words: *resolve* and *passion*.

DANCE TEACHES RESOLVE.

Resolve is your inexhaustible intention to go for what you want and to do so without compromise. It's your steadfast "I'm bigger than any future problem, and can handle what's ahead" state of mind.

The very nature of your dance training has armed you with sensible, everyday, real-world strategies for life beyond the barres of your studio. You are primed for greatness.

If you've ever been in a dance class and believed you were completely depleted, only to hear the teacher say, "Last time, everybody—once more," you'll recall how you summoned endurance and extended yourself beyond what you thought possible. You've lived in that blissful moment where exhaustion and elation exist in one breath. That "do it once more" ability helps you through doubtful times in life when you may have difficulty believing in yourself—but then go forward to either try again or reach for something new.

If you've ever rehearsed an eight-count of choreography over and over and over, you understand unwavering tenacity and determination. That mental toughness and stamina developed from experimenting, revising, clarifying, and breaking down sections into smaller parts. You have firsthand experience in making improvements, learning how to do better, and then turning what works into a habit through faithful practice. Consider the intense hours and weeks you have spent in preparation for the stage. You know how much work gets completed behind closed doors, off the stage, and out of the limelight. You have internal strength driving you in ways unseen by others.

If you've balanced dance education with academics and other activities, you're familiar with time management and goal setting.

If you've judiciously evaluated dance footage of your own fresh, funky moves, you appreciate the value of accountability through honest self-assessment. A healthy awareness of where you stand in relation to all other beings is one of the ultimate skills for lifelong personal growth and learning.

Dance teaches you that it's O.K. to take action without always waiting for fear or anxiety to lift. You walked onstage despite the fright? Resolve did that. If you've ever performed for a live audience, you know how many things are happening at once and how many of them can go wrong. During high-pressure moments, you make split-second decisions about multiple variables, most of which are concealed from the audience. Your nonverbal problem-solving skills serve as testament to your capacity to wing it, revise, and re-stage as necessary. And so goes life.

PASSION MAKES QUITTING NOT AN OPTION.

Passion fuels success. It's the driving force that puts pep in your step and pride in your stride. Passion is the heart and soul energy that lifts your standards, efficiently manages your time, and disciplines your habits.

Passion makes success fun and inevitable, because when you love what you do and you do it well, you feel good about yourself. And, some days, feeling good about yourself *is* success.

If you're having a hard time finding what you're passionate about, research subjects that sound remotely interesting to you. Try new things, keep looking, and keep paying attention. And pay attention to what's got your attention.

You'll know you've hit upon something you're passionate about when you re-prioritize your schedule to spend more time engaged in what you enjoy. (By the way, Julia Cameron's book *The Artist's Way* is a great resource for creative people searching to discover their gifts.)

Passion isn't necessary for success or happiness. It's just nice when passion wakes you up instead of an alarm clock.

SO, WHAT HAVE WE LEARNED FROM ALL THIS?

There's no magic potion or golden ticket for success. Luck, windfalls, having lots of money, knowing the right people, or being in the right place at the right time are factors that certainly come into play. But they don't tell the whole story. The lucky break for many is the culmination of years of hard work.

You want to love your life? Give it your attention. Because what has your focus, energy, and time, has you. You won't know how good the water feels until you jump in. Unleash your creativity. Take a dive. Swim. Release your wings. Fly. Hit the dance floor.

Soar.

THE MARK OF EXCELLENCE IS UPON YOU, AND POSITIVE CHANGE
HAPPENS MINUTE BY MINUTE. AS A MATTER OF FACT,
IT'S HAPPENING RIGHT NOW.

WORKS CITED

Chapter 4. The Splendors of Dance
(1) Verghese, Joe, M.D., Lipton, Richard B., M.D., and Katz, Mindy J., M.P.H. (19 June 2003). Leisure activities and the risk of dementia in the elderly. *The New England Journal of Medicine.* Retrieved on 22 June 2017 from http://www.nejm.org/doi/full/10.1056/NEJMoa022252#t=article.

(2) Center for Online Education. (2016). 10 Salient studies on the importance of art in education. Retrieved on 23 June 2017 from http://www.onlinecolleges.net/10-salient-studies-on-the-arts-in-education/.

(3) Scheuler, Leslie, PhD. (2010). Arts education makes a difference in Missouri schools. Retrieved on 22 June 2017 from https://nasaa-arts.org/wp-content/uploads/2017/06/b657d9f1adfc.pdf.

(4) Dana Foundation. (2009). Neuroeducation: Learning, arts, and the brain. Retrieved on 23 June 2017 from http://www.dana.org/Publications/PublicationDetails.aspx?id=44432.

(5) Krakauer, John. (2008). Why do we like to dance—And move to the beat? Retrieved on 23 June 2017 from https://www.scientificamerican.com/article/experts-dance/.

(6) American Cancer Society. (24 Mar. 2014). Physical activity and the cancer patient. Retrieved on 23 June 2017 from https://www.cancer.org/treatment/survivorship-during-and-after-treatment/staying-active/physical-activity-and-the-cancer-patient.html.

(7) *Berkeley Wellness.* (20 Nov. 2014). The many health benefits of dancing. Retrieved on 23 June 2017 from http://www.berkeleywellness.com/fitness/active-lifestyle/article/many-health-benefits-dancing.

(8) Beris, Rebecca. (1 Mar. 2017). 5 Things that will happen to your brain when you dance. Retrieved on 22 June 2017 from http://www.lifehack.org/374710/5-things-that-will-happen-to-your-brain-when-you-dance.

Chapter 9. Dance as a Way of Life
(1) Robinson, Ken, Sir. (04 Oct. 2014). Dancer needed to move to think. Retrieved on 22 June 2017 from http://www.npr.org/2014/10/04/353679082/dancer-needed-to-move-to-think.

(2) Eichenbaum, Rose, & Barnes, Clive. *Masters of Movement: Portraits of America's Great Choreographers.* Washington: Smithsonian, 2007. Print.

Chapter 11. Auditioning
(1) Paula Abdul reveals 30-year secret. (31 Jan. 2014). Retrieved on 22 June 2017 from https://www.webpronews.com/paula-abdul-reveals-30-year-secret-2014-01/.